"Life is a mess of our sin and suffering, but thankfully God meets us with his redeeming grace. Instead of judgment and rejection, he offers love and acceptance. Kimm unpacks the wonder of God's mercy with honesty and courage and shows how it reaches all the way down to every dimension of our hearts and lives."

Justin S. Holcomb, professor at Gordon-Conwell Theological Seminary, author of *On the Grace of God*

"What a refreshing book! *Beloved Mess* is funny, arresting, radical, and best of all, true. Sometimes I think we Christians have missed the "main thing" about our faith: We're great sinners and Jesus is a great Savior. That means that we're free, forgiven, acceptable, and loved. If that doesn't make you want to dance, laugh, and sing, you're dead and just haven't been buried yet. Read this book and give it to all your friends. We'll laugh, sing, and dance together."

Steve Brown, broadcaster, seminary professor, and author

"In *Beloved Mess*, Kimm pours out her heart with a gospel urgency and authenticity that brings you to your knees in praise of God's glorious grace. There is no faking it or tidying up of her story. She believes God's love for each of us in our mess is the most beautiful thing we can behold, and she puts it on full display. Read this short but life-changing book, go back to it again and again, and see yourself falling more in love with the One who loved us and gave himself for us."

Jessica Thompson, author of *Everyday Grace*

"Tired of performance-based, score-carding, joy-sabotaging, heart-deflating spirituality? Me too. My friend Kimm Crandall gives voice to the longing of our hearts for less posing and more reposing in the outrageous riches of God's grace. *Beloved Mess* underscores that it is our 'belovedness' in Jesus which frees us from our navel-gazing fixation with ourselves and leads us into a life of living and loving to the glory of God. Kimm has reminded me afresh that it was *never* about the 'victorious Christian life,' but about the victorious Christ. It's precisely because God *cannot* love us any more than he already does in Christ that we can think *less often* about ourselves, and *more often* about extending his mercy and grace to others."

Scotty Ward Smith, teacher in residence at West End Community Church, author of *Every Season Prayers*

"Kimm Crandall couldn't hide her mess if she tried, and it's the most beloved thing I know about her. Kimm, in life and in this book, displays her glorious need for the gospel and its good grace. She clings to the cross and teaches her readers how to live with vulnerability toward Christ and others. It's a refreshing mess if I ever saw one."

Lore Ferguson Wilbert, director of community and formation at Park Church, Denver, writer at Sayable.net

GOD'S
PERFECT
LOVE
FOR YOUR
IMPERFECT
LIFE

KIMM **CRANDALL**

BakerBooks

a division of Baker Publishing Group
Grand Rapids, Michigan

Published by Baker Books
a division of Baker Publishing Group
P.O. Box 6287, Grand Rapids, MI 49516–6287
www.bakerbooks.com

Printed in the United States of America

Library of Congress Cataloging-in-Publication Data
Names: Crandall, Kimm, 1974– author.
Title: Beloved mess : God's perfect love for your imperfect life / Kimm Crandall.
Description: Grand Rapids : Baker Books, 2016. | Includes bibliographical references.
Identifiers: LCCN 2016001490 | ISBN 9780801019005 (pbk.)
Subjects: LCSH: God (Christianity)—Love. | Grace (Theology)
Classification: LCC BT140 .C73 2016 | DDC 248.4—dc23
LC record available at http://lccn.loc.gov/2016001490

The author is represented by the literary agency of Wolgemuth & Associates, Inc.

Some names and details have been changed to protect the privacy of the individuals involved.

16 17 18 19 20 21 22   7 6 5 4 3 2 1

To my husband, Justin:

my best friend, fellow grace moocher,
and dance floor virtuoso.

Thank you for loving me as I am.

Contents

Foreword

Kimm Crandall is a friend of mine. But it's not always been that way. There was a time when Kimm didn't really like me and because, like her, I thrive on acceptance and sensed her displeasure, I'm not sure I liked her either. But thankfully all of that has changed.

There was a time when I thought and spoke almost exclusively about how to be good. I even wrote about how to get better at being good. But then grace came crashing into my life. Not because I had some great fall into unspeakable immorality and knew that I couldn't get better—no, actually I thought I was getting better. I thought I was excelling, doing my best, being faithful and obedient, and I knew how to tell other people how to be like me. Unlike others who talk about grace, I didn't go through one of those darkened-room, curled-up-in-the-fetal-position experiences. No, what I went through was something less dramatic, more gradual, but utterly Copernican in its transformation. It was a slow stripping away of my self-righteousness and self-confidence, a reorienting of my life away from my own perceived goodness and toward Jesus's perfection.

Here's how it went: In the church I was attending, I had friends (one in particular) who kept harping on me and telling me that I was already pleasing to God, that I really wasn't living in light of the gospel by focusing on how to be good. But I didn't immediately embrace the wonder of grace like someone who had found lost treasure. No, I resisted it. I went kicking and screaming down that road. *Grace? Freedom? Rest? Love? No way! Not me! I am a serious Christian, a serious theologian. I have a Master's degree in biblical counseling for crying out loud!* I can't tell you how angry these "gospel" people made me. *You think I don't understand the gospel? You think I don't live in the light of grace? How dare you!* These were thoughts that, like little pieces of sand, stuck in my heart and maddened and irritated me until Jesus finally formed a gospel pearl. His message of love began to wear down my resistance to it, to him, until I began to see beauty and love and yes, grace.

Eventually I found myself hungry to seriously investigate what these "gospel" people were talking about, and I wrote *Because He Loves Me*, and that, as they say, was pretty much the end of the story. I became aware of how self-righteous, angry, critical, and demanding I was. I knew that I didn't really love people and that the gifts of insight and wisdom Jesus had given me had been used by me for self-promotion and harshness. The light began to dawn. I was in great need of grace, and all the more so because I didn't think I was.

Then Kimm and I became friends. She attended a conference where I spoke on grace, and she glared at me through most of it. I understand why she glared. There was a big part of me that still wanted to glare at grace.

In the Lord's kind providence, we started to attend the same church and ended up in the same home group. Our friendship was inevitable because it was all too apparent that we were both in the same boat. I was (in using that past-tense verb, I flatter myself) both proud and self-righteous but also desperate for grace, and I wanted to learn to love the weak. I was finally starting to be able to admit the truth about myself and not be terrified when others pointed it out. Kimm was desperate like me. Her life was in shambles and she was coming to see that because she'd built it on her ability to excel, to be the best, to be anything but second, she was destined for misery. Her first-place-ness idol was destroying her. She needed grace. She needed to hear grace and taste grace and listen to grace over and over and over again. I needed to give it. She needed to hear it. We became good friends.

Through the years our friendship has deepened and grown. We've both grown in our understanding and confidence of God's love for us in Christ, and we've come to identify ourselves as desperate sinners, loved by a great and kind Savior. We've laughed together and cried together and been seriously angry together. But through it all she continually reminds me about God's love for me and encourages me nonstop to bring freedom (or "drop keys," as she says) for desperate prisoners wherever I go. I'm deeply grateful for her prayer and encouragement.

Kimm is eminently qualified to talk to you about being a beloved mess. That's because, like me, she is one. But please note that she isn't just a "mess." She's a *beloved* mess; she is one of her Lord's dear sweeties and she knows how to talk about that simply because she's had to tell it to herself over and over again.

So, I give to you *Beloved Mess* and my friend Kimm. I hope you enjoy her and her message of grace as much as I do. I'm learning that the more I think I understand my Father's love for me in Christ, the farther I am from understanding it at all. This book will help. I'm so grateful for it and for Kimm. She's my friend. She's yours too.

Elyse Fitzpatrick, author of *Because He Loves Me: How Christ Transforms Our Daily Life*

Introduction

A little bit messy. A little bit ruined. A beautiful disaster.
Just like me.

Michelle Hodkin

Real life is only ever just real life. Messy. What it means
depends on how you look at it. The only thing you've got
to do is find a way to live there.

Patrick Ness

Nobody's perfect. Well, there was this one guy, but we killed
him.

Christopher Moore

There is an area of our property that I often visit when I am hiding from my kids. Maybe I have an important phone call that I
don't want them to overhear, or maybe I have just blown up at the
entire household and need a place to escape to so that I will not
do any more damage. Sometimes I just need to be alone so I can

eat chocolate or shed a few tears. Whatever the case may be, it is my refuge. It's a part of our three acres that makes me happy.

In this little corner of our property resides a giant oak tree, an old garden that once flourished as the place for a wedding of the previous owners, and an aviary that was the home of what I imagine were some beautiful and well-loved birds.

I often find myself thinking about what this area once looked like. I saw glimpses of it when the house was on the market, as it had been maintained far above the standard that we have kept for it. And I briefly saw a picture of the wedding that was held there before we took ownership. But when I look around at the neglected landscape in its current state, I can't imagine that it was ever fit for such a celebration. It's a mess.

The majestic oak tree houses a broken swing, and its branches overarch a litter of lawn chairs that my kids have dragged underneath and left overturned. The landscape gravel that had been laboriously shoveled and spread about is now covered in a thick layer of leaves with random weeds popping through. The planters that were once carefully arranged with perennials are now overgrown with stalky plants. The aviary has been taken over by my kids and is now used as a clubhouse, with books, blankets, and Christmas lights strewn about in the fashion of novice decorators. It is imperfect to say the least.

As I look around my garden area, I see chaos. I see a jumble of what was once a place beautiful and perfect enough to have the honor of being a wedding venue. But I can also see fragments of what it once was: the arbor that the happy couple exchanged vows beneath, the rocks that neatly line the beds that were once filled with colorful flowers. I imagine the birds singing in their aviary, happy for the California sunshine. I see glimpses of what once was, and this frustrates me because I know that as busy as my life is with four kids, I will never be able to restore the beauty of it all.

I venture to guess that most of you have picked up this book because you are tired of being a mess. You are tired of not being okay. You are frustrated knowing that, like my garden, your perfection will not be fully realized this side of heaven. Maybe you even fear that God is disappointed in you because you can't seem to clean yourself up.

Perhaps you have worked feverishly to try to make yourself okay. After all, the Christian culture tells us that if we would just read more, pray more, and cuss less we will experience transformation and finally live the victorious Christian life that we were meant to live. But for you, nothing seems to be changing. The weeds just keep popping back up. Nothing seems to make the untidiness go away. You are told that if you just cling tighter to the cross, you will experience peace and joy, but at this point you don't even have the strength to lift your arms.

You love Jesus. You want to do what he commands, but every step you take feels like failure. To you, the Christian life seems more like a miserable version of the children's board game Chutes and Ladders. With every success you climb the ladder toward God, and with every failure you slide down the dreaded chute farther away from him. You are ready to flip the game board over, sending all of the other players' pieces into the air, fitfully declaring, "I quit!"

You are not alone.

This book was written for people who are ready to quit because they can't handle the mess. People like my friend Charles who struggles with addiction and depression. He loves God and desires to do what is right, but he finds it hard to believe that he is loved by God, partly because the church and his own family have cast him aside. His brokenness consumes him. He knows what God's law says about his struggles and he lives under its crushing weight, but he has never had anyone show him how the gospel speaks into his mess. He needs to know that he isn't alone in his struggles and that the grace of God sets him free to be loved as he is.

And it was written for people like Katie, a homeschooling mom of six. From the outside she appears to have it all together. Her children are well behaved, and she is often praised for her performance as a godly mother and wife. But the secret that nobody knows is that Katie is dying on the inside. She constantly feels like a failure as a wife, mother, and Christian woman. Although she loves the praise she receives from those around her, she wishes her real life could somehow be exposed. She is exhausted from keeping up appearances, but she is also afraid to share her pain with anyone. She tries harder to please God with her good works, hoping that somehow he too cannot see through the glittering image that she has created for herself. Katie needs to know that the gospel sets her free to expose her mess to others. She needs to know that she is not alone and that she can rest in Christ's love for her.

Beloved Mess is for doubters like Charles, for those who have lost hope that they could ever be good enough, for those who need to know that the strength of their faith is not the object of their faith. It's for those who are just barely hanging on. It's for those who have been asked the crushing question, "What are you doing for God today?" and have no answer.

It's for others as well. It's for the "good girls and boys" who have thought that their performance impresses God. It's for the merit mongers, performance addicts, and approval junkies. It's for those who always have an answer to what they have done for God today and are happy to provide you with their list. It's for those, like Katie, who have buried their mess so deep that they have made an imposter of their outer selves, fearful that one day their authentic selves might be exposed.

Beloved Mess is about the hard work of believing that we are his Beloved. It's about living in our belovedness, resting in our sweet security with Christ, and truly believing that because of Christ we really are loved just as we are. It's about the good news of the gospel sidelining the bad news of our humanity.

I will begin this book by showing you that I am just as much of a mess as you are. We'll explore the purpose of the law in the life of the believer. I will introduce you to my imposter, who I am sure is friends with yours. I'll seek to answer the question, why? Why is it okay to not be okay? How can we be loved just as we are if we were made to be image bearers of the God who said, "Be perfect, as your heavenly Father is perfect" (Matt. 5:48)? But don't worry, I won't leave you crushed by the law, feeling like a failure. Eventually, I will let loose a cannon of good news that will bring you hope. And in case you haven't had enough Jesus, I will help you to see what it means to live the life of the Beloved and finally leave you kissed by grace.

At the end of each chapter I have included reflection questions to help you as you travel through this book. Journey through it on your own, grab a friend, or grab a gaggle of friends. Discuss it. Struggle through it. Ask God to speak his love over you in ways that prove that you indeed are his Beloved.

My hope is that throughout this book you will see that it's okay that you aren't okay. In fact, it is my hope that you will begin to see how much you are loved in the midst of your mess and how it cannot separate you from God.

I'm a Mess

The Good News of the gospel of grace cries out: We are all, equally, privileged but unentitled beggars at the door of God's mercy.

Brennan Manning

Real life is messy, inconsistent, and it's seldom when anything ever really gets resolved. It's taken me a long time to realize that.

Alan Moore

"Have no fear of this mess," said the Cat in the Hat.

Dr. Seuss

I'm a mess. I really am. I'm not talking about my physical environment—the crumbs you will find in my butter or the laundry piles that spill out of every closet in my house. I'm speaking of my heart; a heart that struggles with the reality of living between the already and the not yet; a heart that lives with the tension of being here on earth, struggling against my selfish desires, yet longing to be in heaven, the place that holds my true citizenship.

As I grow and mature spiritually, I don't see myself as less of a mess but more of one. The older I get, the more I need approval. (I am an approval addict.) The wiser I become, the more I long for people to tell me how wise I am. The more opportunity I have, the less sure I am of myself. I rely heavily on my performance to justify myself and find worth. I am a performance junkie. I often find myself trying to earn God's favor by showing him how good I can be (as if he didn't already know my motives). I am a merit monger.[1] I am obsessive. I mean *really* obsessive. Just ask my friends. One friend told me that I am not happy unless I am freaking out over something. She's right.

I have overactive guilt glands. Everything in my life seems to be filtered through shame and false guilt, often leaving me guessing as to whether I should be repenting and apologizing or checking myself into the local psych ward.

Speaking of that, there is the depression. Oh, the depression. It hits me like a knife in the back, leaving me on my knees gasping for air. I feel as though I am constantly running from the darkness. Every so often I trip, and it covers me like a wet woolen blanket, so dank and dark that I don't have the strength to wiggle my way out from under it. There have been times of darkness in my life when I thought that the world would be a better place without me. I stashed away pills, waiting for the right time to slip quietly off without having to worry about waking up and facing the harshness of the cruel world.

I have withheld food from myself in an attempt to seek control, and I have binged and purged to try to cope with what I could not. I have cut and burned my body as a way to deal with the pain, hiding my scars from others, wondering what they would think of me if they only knew the truth, all while trying to be the model mother to my four children.

And as if my inner mess is not enough, there is the way I have treated my family. I have lashed out at them for stupid things; I have joined in on the petty fights and I can throw an attitude with the best of teenage daughters. I have been unkind, selfish, rude, and downright ugly. I have put myself before them and have not loved them the way that God intended for a mother to love. I have failed to show compassion when it was most needed, and you do *not* want to hear the things that have come out of my mouth upon being woken up from a nap. I have lived for the approval of my kids; I have used them to make myself look good and I have chastised them for making me look bad. I have shared my disappointment in them when they did not fulfill my expectations and have put ridiculous amounts of pressure on them to perform. I have twisted Scripture to get them to obey. I have manipulated them with my words. I have been angry, oh so angry. I have yelled and have unfairly disciplined. I have treated them with harshness. I have failed them more times than I want to admit, and yet they still love me.

That is grace.

Your pain may be different from mine. You may not struggle with the terrifying darkness of depression or the overwhelming fear of anxiety. You may not punish yourself the way that I do when things get too much for you to handle. Maybe you are more prone to numb yourself in front of the television and polish off an entire box of cookies in one sitting, or work out obsessively to push away the pain of life, or hide your fears behind long work hours and career advancement. In any case we all have our own burdens of dysfunction. Some of it is caused by our own sin. Yet some is a result of our woundedness—a result of the sin of others against us. But in the end, whether it's our sin or our circumstances, we are all in need of the same thing: to be known and loved as we are, right *where* we are.

If you are wondering why I seem to have such poor self-esteem and are worried about my negativity, don't be. Let me assure you that I could go on for just as long with a list of my accomplishments and the ways that I am a great mom and a valuable asset to the world. (Yes, I really do think about myself this much.)

And if you are worried that I am bragging about or condoning sin when I speak of the ways that I have failed, you can relax. Every one of these failures has brought great grief over my disobedience and a longing to see Jesus through the thickness of what threatens to suffocate me with condemnation. In every one of these moments the law exposes my need to be rescued. In every one of these moments grace floods in, an outrageous act of love for this undeserving sinner. I have a great Savior whose grace long outlasts my failings. A Savior who has taken each item of my mess, each thing on my list (and yours as well), and has splattered his blood upon them, making atonement for us, pleading our destitute case in the heavenly throne room of grace.

You may be wondering why I would start a book with a long list of my personal failures and weaknesses. Maybe you think I'm crazy to put myself out there like this, to be so brutally honest. This has come from a promise to myself a few years back. I decided that I would not speak or write to an audience without first proving to them that I was a sinner.[2] You see, it's not enough for me to hear that someone else is "not perfect" or is "a sinner just like me." I need proof! I need to know that the person speaking to me has been in my shoes. I need to know that he or she understands what it is to be a sinner and stand in desperate need of grace like I do. I need to know that other Christians are not the shiny, happy people that my mind wants to trick me into believing they are.

So, I'm going to assume that you feel the same as I do. Does it not bring you a sigh of relief when someone who you may think has it all together suddenly proves that she does not? Admit it, when you see a highly acclaimed actor trip on his way to the stage to receive a prestigious award, you and I both have a sudden burst of freedom that reassures us that he is just like us. Or what about when you glimpse those seemingly perfect parents at the park lose their temper as they load their crying children into their minivans. You can almost hear the sound of your cage door unlocking, and you want to go and thank them for falling apart (although they might think you are crazy).

We want the comfort of knowing that everyone else is just like us. We want to know that we are not alone.

Met in Our Mess

"We just want you to know what you will be getting if we join your church. We are both a bit of a mess." My husband voiced these words from a place of courage as we sat across from two pastors in the corner booth of our local diner. We had moved to our small town several months prior and believed that it was finally time to make the switch to a church in our own community. But with both of us in counseling for severe depression and marital problems, we were afraid our mess would be too much to bring to a new congregation. Pride and fear had left us undecided about making the change for months.

As I sat staring into my coffee and rearranging the eggs on my plate, I was glad for what he said, but the shame had paralyzed me once again. I couldn't look into those men's eyes for fear of their judgment. I sat anticipating the stab of rejection.

To my amazement, judgment and rejection were the furthest words from their lips. We were met with nothing but love and acceptance. The pastors had already been aware of our struggles. They had already inquired about us with our previous pastor and knew far more than we had planned on exposing, yet there was only room for grace on their lips. We were already known, yet loved and accepted when we feared that being known would mean judgment and rejection. The words "We know about your mess. We love you. You are welcome here" were the most curative words that two hearts crushed by the law could hear at that moment. No longer did we simply feel tolerated; we now felt desired.

This conversation was only the beginning of our journey into learning that life is messy, each one of us is broken, and to live in a messy and broken world means we all need grace. It was a beautiful example of how God's one-way love comes down through Christ and meets us in our mess. It is only through Christ that we can be both fully known and fully loved. The law threatens judgment and rejection while the gospel tells us the beautiful story of a loving God who came to free us from shame; a God who saw that we were a mess, and through one act of outrageous grace met us in our mess with love and acceptance. And every day since that marvelous, tragic, sacrificial, life-giving act he has pursued us all for the sake of love.

Through all of my mess, past and present, God has shown me that the Christian life is not about the good things I do. It's not about my performance, my perfection, or giving up my life for Christ. It is about Christ's performance, perfection, and giving of himself *for me* because I just can't get it right. It's all about Christ *for me*.

Unfortunately, when we spill our junk out onto the greasy diner tables of life, much of the time we are not met with this kind of love and acceptance.

The only way I can be so vulnerable with you is because of the gospel. If the gospel really is rescue for sinners (which it is), we should be able to freely admit our messiness. That's what sinners are—messes.[3]

How This Book Is Different

What makes this book different from other material that you will read on the Christian life is this: I am not going to focus on telling you how to be a better you, how to find the beauty in parenting, how to embrace your calling as a spouse, or how I have fixed all of my mess by social-media fasting and thirty-day challenges. I'm not going to pretend to have it all together and give you a list of ways to be like me (and after what you have just read, I'm sure you are thankful for that). It would be easy for me to write a book that simply states that it's okay to not be perfect. But our hope is not in the fact that we are imperfect, it's in the fact that *Christ* is perfect in our stead. That is why the words "nobody's perfect" are only freeing in the moment. Because we know, deep down, that we were made in the image of perfection. God's law calls us to be holy as he is holy. And so there is no rest until we find that perfection.

What you need to hear from me is that I am a mess, you are a mess, *and* that there is hope outside of ourselves; a hope in the one who came and lived perfectly on our behalf because he knew that we would make a huge mess out of what we have been given. He knew that it would be impossible for us to consistently love others, so he came and he loved. He loved deeper than you can imagine, without even an unloving thought for anyone around him, no matter how they treated him. He knew that you would be irritated with all the bad drivers in your way, the cattiness of your co-workers, and the drama of your family. So he came. He came and he patiently endured those around him. Those who constantly dropped the ball, upset the

> What you need to hear from me is that I am a mess, you are a mess, **and** that there is hope outside of ourselves; a hope in the one who came and lived perfectly on our behalf because he knew that we would make a huge mess out of what we have been given.

basket, and pushed their way to the front of the line. He came for messes like you and me.

When we think of our past, present, and possible future messes, we can have hope. Not the hope that we will someday be able to muster up the strength to be better people, but the hope that God is changing us and that—whatever state we are in, whether a state of grace or disgrace—we have been washed in the blood of the one who knows us and loves us as we are, the one who makes us okay. We remain his Beloved. As Simon Tugwell said,

> Whatever past achievements might bring us honor, whatever past disgraces might make us blush, all have been crucified with Christ and exist no more except in the deep recesses of eternity, where "good is enhanced into glory and evil miraculously established as part of the greater good."[4]

I want to show you just how important a role the gospel plays in your everyday life. I'll talk about grace, grace, and more grace. Not a "God looks the other way" kind of grace (which is a common misunderstanding of grace), but rather the grace of the gospel. Grace is not about God looking the other way but rather about him looking directly at us and seeing every good work that his Son has done on our behalf. Grace sustains us in our mess; it makes it possible to be loved as we are. This is a scandalous grace. The truth is that we are all scandalously messy, just as Mike Yaconelli heralds in his incredibly freeing book, *Messy Spirituality*.

> What landed Jesus on the cross was the preposterous idea that common, ordinary, broken, screwed-up people *could be godly!* What drove Jesus's enemies crazy were his criticisms of the "perfect" religious people and his acceptance of the imperfect nonreligious people. The shocking implication of Jesus's ministry is that *anyone* can be spiritual.

Scandalous? Maybe.

Maybe truth *is* scandalous. Maybe the scandal is that all of us are in some condition of not-togetherness, even those of us who are trying to be godly. Maybe we're all a mess, not only sinfully messy but inconsistently messy, up-and-down messy, in-and-out messy, I-understand-uh-now-I-don't-understand messy.[5]

As we walk hand in hand through these pages, through our messes, the only real and lasting encouragement that I can give to you is to remind you that Jesus has redeemed you from the mess that you have been, the mess that you are, and the messes that you will make in the future.

I refuse to give you ten steps to overcome your challenges, and I'm not going to tell you that freedom is found in the fact that "nobody's perfect." Nor am I going to tell you that "to err is human" and that as long as you are trying you are okay with God. That's not the gospel! That's not good news! The gospel is this: *You were made to be perfect. The law requires you to be perfect, but you can't be. Christ was perfect on your behalf, thus silencing the law's voice toward you. You are free!*

> Grace is not about God looking the other way but rather about him looking directly at us and seeing every good work that his Son has done on our behalf. Grace sustains us in our mess; it makes it possible to be loved as we are. This is a scandalous grace.

You may find that my honesty is a stretch for you. Maybe you would never say you're a mess, or you don't see yourself as *that bad* of a person. Perhaps you find it easier to pursue the "try harder, do better" avenue of Christianity because it gives you a sense of hope that you will someday get it right (or at least get it a bit better than it is right now). If my honesty doesn't impress you, I understand. But please stick with me. There is so much more to be discovered here. Though you may believe that you are doing okay, I hope that you will see that you are no different than I am. The law condemns us all. We all need Jesus.

On the other hand, maybe you can relate to and embrace all I have said. Maybe you are nodding your head in agreement with this list and even adding to it. Perhaps you are relieved to hear that you don't have to be perfect and that it's okay to just be who you are.

But let's not stop there. Join me as I delve deeper into how it is possible to be loved just as we are in the midst of all of our ugliness. I think you will find hope in these pages as I prove to you the truth of the gospel—the truth that we are all his Beloved Messes.

Henri Nouwen beautifully captures the cry of each one of our messy hearts and the hope we have within the pain of our brokenness when he says:

> To us, who cry out from the depth of our brokenness for a hand that will touch us, an arm that can embrace us, lips that will kiss us, a word that speaks to us here and now, and a heart that is not afraid of our fears and tremblings; to us, who feel our own pain as no other human being feels it, has felt it, or ever will feel it and who are always waiting for someone who dares to come close—to us a person has come who could truly say, 'I am with you.' Jesus Christ is God-with-us. . . . Our human pain reverberates in his innermost self.[6]

FOR THE JOURNEY

1. As you read this chapter what was your initial reaction to the author's confession of sin and the sharing of her messiness? Were you shocked or comforted? Explain your response.

2. Do you find it difficult to share your mess with others? Why or why not?

3. What are you hoping that God will reveal to you as you work through this book?

The League of the Guilty

Until we admit we are a mess, Jesus won't have anything to do with us. Once we admit how unlovely we are, how unattractive we are, how lost we are, Jesus shows up unexpectedly.

Mike Yaconelli

We're the league of the guilty, after all, not the league of the shortly-to-become-good. We are a work in progress. We will always be a work in progress. We will always fail, and it will always matter.

Francis Spufford

You may have thought it was incredibly brave of me to lay out my mess for you the way that I did in chapter 1. And perhaps you have constructed some superhero image of me based on my transparency. If so, let that go. I'm no hero. No, I am a broken sinner who has nothing left but the strength of Christ to stand on.

I have nothing to prove to you except that I am a great sinner who needs a great Savior. But it wasn't always this way.

Second Place Is the First Loser

The majority of my life has been spent running from the reality of my heart, shoving down every painful thought and memory, to turn to something, anything, that would make me feel better. I compensated for my lack of emotional strength with physical strength and athleticism. I put all of my hope into sports. Everything was a competition, and I was driven by my life's motto: "Second place is the first loser." I lived by the law that told me that failure was not an option, and so I became really good at being really good.

Once I became a mother I began to realize that I was no longer the star player on the court. There was no formula for success in motherhood. Motherhood was an entirely different game, and I didn't have the skills or talent for it. I was daily confronted with messes, whether it was the cereal that wasn't properly cleaned up from breakfast (and that now seemed to be glued to the countertop) or the glitter that resided in the crevasses of the wood floor from the "crafts" that my kids made the previous Christmas. The battle to keep my kids clean, my house clean, and myself clean was never ending.

So I did the only thing that I knew how to do: I worked harder. I was going to be the best mother there ever was. Not only that, I was going to be the godliest mother as well. So I studied all the parenting books and blogs I could find. I took in all I could from the older mothers around me, questioning them on why and how they did what they did.[1] I was training myself to become what I thought was the #1 Mom.

But I could never seem to get there. I could see the trophy off in the distance, but as I ran toward it the hurdles seemed to grow taller and wider, and falling began to hurt more and more. One day I just couldn't get up.

After my fourth child was born, I went from the coveted star player position to not even making the cut. God broke me, and it was the best thing that ever happened to me. I had gone from a self-righteous woman who loved to tell others how they could be good (just like her) if they just tried harder, to a basket case of a mom lying on the floor of her bathroom with a fistful of pills.

This was the beginning of my journey into learning that to be alive is to be imperfect—messy, even. Up until then I really did think that if I just tried hard enough, I could move closer and closer to the perfection I so desperately longed for. But Christianity isn't about being less of a mess; it's about admitting that we need to be saved from trying to clean ourselves up. It is by God's grace that my wreckage was exposed. It was his kindness that led me to repent of my pursuit of perfection. But it took me almost ending my life with a hidden stash of pain medication and sleeping pills to show me how broken I really was. Years of junk shoved deep into the recesses of my heart were now spewing forth for all to see. And though I had been a Christian for many years, I had not quite understood my need for Jesus.

> But Christianity isn't about being less of a mess; it's about admitting that we need to be saved from trying to clean ourselves up.

The Law's Crushing Demands

Unfortunately this is the case for many believers. We claim to love Jesus, but we have left him behind in our pursuit of holiness. We often believe that it is up to us to secure God's love by doing all that God commands. We have misunderstood the use of the law and have lost sight of why Jesus had to come and die. That is why it is imperative that we allow the law to do its work: to show us our need for a Rescuer.

Before my breakdown (and even now at times) I believed that if I just followed the rules, or rather the "little l" law of what the world around me was saying that I needed to be, then I would be okay. I'd follow all the "good mom" and "amazing wife" laws that promised if I just diapered, cooked, dressed, and schooled a certain way, then I'd have obedient kids, a magazine cover–worthy house, and amazing sex.

> I'd follow all the "good mom" and "amazing wife" laws that promised if I just diapered, cooked, dressed, and schooled a certain way, then I'd have obedient kids, a magazine cover-worthy house, and amazing sex.

The "little l" law, or what I like to call experiential law, is all of those things around us that are constantly laying burdens on us to try harder and do better. The pressure of the experiential law can come in the form of blog posts suggesting that if we follow their list of ten ways to be happy, then our depression will dissipate and our lives will be transformed. Or the Pinterest post that promises us that our unwanted fat will melt away if we follow their special superfood, paleo, gluten-free, chia-infused, homemade organic water recipe. It comes from the magazine rack where we read about three ways to achieve amazing orgasms (*guaranteed!*) on the front covers of multiple publications as we stand in line with our kids, hoping they don't ask what the "Big O" is on the car ride home. Or from the television that is blaring at us all the ways that we too need to be rich, young, and beautiful, followed by commercials that promise us prosperity, health, and happiness if we buy their products.

Do you see what I mean here? If you really begin to look around, you will see all the ways that it is possible to fail to live up to the expectations of the world or even perhaps the expectations that we put on ourselves in just one day. Like modern-day Pharisees we create "little l" laws to make the "big L" law—the commands of God's law—seem achievable. We may know that we can't fulfill God's law so we get busy trying to fulfill whatever grants us self-approval, trying to convince ourselves that we really aren't *that bad*.

I also believed during that time (and often still catch myself believing) that if I could just obey the "big L" law, then I would make God happy. If I could just obey everything that God required of me, then I'd be okay. The problem was that I didn't understand the depths of God's law. I didn't understand that it wasn't created for me to fulfill it; it was meant for me to fail it. The standard was purposefully set way out of my reach so that I would know how very much I needed Jesus.

> The problem was that I didn't understand the depths of God's law. I didn't understand that it wasn't created for me to fulfill it; it was meant for me to fail it.

Up until my breakdown I honestly thought I was doing pretty well with the "big L" laws. The Ten Commandments? No prob! I wasn't murdering, stealing, or having an affair. I wasn't lying; just not telling the whole truth. I wasn't coveting my neighbor's wife; I was just wishing that I could be more like her. I hadn't murdered anyone; I just had thoughts of how much better off my life would be without certain people. What I didn't understand was that God's law required me to obey in thought, word, *and* deed. It wasn't until I crashed and burned at fulfilling all of the "little l" laws around me that I began to see that I was even farther from fulfilling the "big L" laws.

And when my life came plummeting down in depression, marital dysfunction, anxiety, eating disorders, self-injury, and suicide plans, God began to show me just how very much I needed someone other than myself to save me. I needed to be rescued from the demands of *both* the experiential laws as well as God's law. I needed to be rescued from myself and from my belief that if I just tried hard enough I would be okay.

It's a struggle for any of us to believe that we are a mess, especially when we seem to be doing all the right things. But the fact is that we all have dirt. There are skeletons in each one of our closets that the law calls out of hiding. Jesus is speaking to each one of us with the same strong words that he used with the Pharisees, whose behavior he detested: "Woe to you, scribes and Pharisees, hypocrites! For you are like whitewashed tombs, which outwardly appear beautiful, but within are full of dead people's bones and all uncleanness" (Matt. 23:27). Our reaction is often one of disbelief and self-defense. It's tough to admit that we really are *that bad.* We are constantly trying to justify ourselves, digging down deep to find something of ourselves that we can call good, but the reality is that not one of us is pulling it off the way we think we are. Not one of us is good apart from Christ.

Throughout this book when I refer to the law it will be an intermingling of experiential law and God's law, because these two types of law often go hand in hand. If I were to only speak about the law in terms of God's law, you might wonder what it is that I am saying that has to do with the mess of everyday life. And if I speak of the law only in terms of experiential law, then you may wonder what any of that has to do with God. Both forms of the law put conditions on us. They both yell, "Try harder! Do better!" with their guarantees of "If you do this, then you will get this." They both expose our need for a Savior.

How the Law Functions

I am reminded of how the law works when I stand in my kitchen on a sunny Southern California afternoon. The sunlight floods my home through our large sliding glass doors and extended windows with such intensity that I often have to wear my sunglasses. I love the light that comes in as the afternoon fades. It brightens our house during a time of homework and after-school exhaustion.

However, the extra light also shows every nose print, handprint, tongue print, and smudge of who-knows-what on our wall of windows. It uncovers every spot on the floor that I thought was clean. It highlights all the dust flying through the air, visible in heavy specks waiting to settle on my furniture. All of my home's hidden dirt is exposed. What I thought was clean really isn't.

We would all agree that having winter afternoon sunlight streaming through our windows, lighting up the room, and warming our home is a delightful gift. I'm thankful for the sunshine, but it also reveals the dirt that my eye did not see without its help. If it weren't shining so intensely into my home, I'd be content with my streaked windows and dusty floors, never seeing their true state.

Just like the sunshine, the law is also a revealer. The law is used to uncover every single way that we have failed. The law is like a beacon of sunlight tracking down every particle of dust that we thought we had taken care of. Every smudge of bitterness, every crumb of impatience that we think we are hiding is exposed for the ugliness it is. We think we are okay until the law enters in. And this is a good thing. Without the law we would not be aware of where we fail and of our need for rescue. The law is meant to scare us, to leave us shaking in our boots, paralyzed with fear of failure and of the eternal consequences that ensue.

But the value of the law stops there. It must stay in its proper place and not cross over the line. As seminary professor and author John T. Pless notes, "The law tells us what we must do, but it is impotent to redeem us from its demands. The law speaks to our works, always showing that even the best of them are tainted with the fingerprints of our sin and insufficient for our salvation."[2]

> The only work that the law can do is to expose our mess and bring us to our knees, begging for grace. But it goes no further. Its work stops there.

It is important that we understand the law in this way, because without the law's demands the gospel loses its luster and simply becomes a nice story. The function of the law is to make us desperate for Jesus. The law cannot save us, nor can it change our hearts. The only work that the law can do is to expose our mess and bring us to our knees, begging for grace. But it goes no further. Its work stops there.

Bringing Us to Our Knees

I don't know about you, but the fact that God requires perfection frightens the heck out of me! Why? Because I know how very bad I really am and how very short I fall in fulfilling the requirements of God's law. It should scare you too. Our propensity for wrongdoing is the very reason why we need the gospel; we need to be rescued from our badness!

The law is meant to terrify the conscience so that it looks to Christ. We must know how very bad off we really are before we can understand how good the grace of God really is. If we do not know what we are being saved from, then the rescue will seem unnecessary. We won't appreciate being set free unless we are aware of the shackles that have imprisoned us.

The law is not meant to be used as a step stool to bring us closer to God. It's not a ladder of good works that we climb to get ourselves to heaven. It doesn't motivate us to love or to serve or to be a better person. The law only makes demands that we cannot fulfill.

The law demands good things such as, "Love the Lord your God with all your heart and with all your soul and with all your mind" and "Love your neighbor as yourself,"[3] but doing these things cannot save us. For that, the law demands perfection. And if you are honest with yourself, you know that you cannot keep it perfectly. After all, when is the last time you loved someone perfectly? Okay, so you loved that person perfectly . . . but for how long? To love perfectly means loving this way all the time. And when you recognized that you loved that person, what did your heart do? Did you proudly pat yourself on the back? I know I do. You see, we cannot escape the law that holds us accountable to perfection. When I try to fulfill its demands, I am found curled up in a ball in the corner crying, "I can't do it. Make it stop!"

> We must know how very bad off we really are before we can understand how good the grace of God really is. If we do not know what we are being saved from, then the rescue will seem unnecessary.

So what are we to do? What are we to do with this law that hunts us down and threatens death? Chuck it out the window, hoping it never finds its way back to us? Pretend it doesn't exist?

In Romans 7:7 Paul writes "What then shall we say? That the law is sin? By no means! Yet if it had not been for the law, I would not have known sin. For I would not have known what it is to covet if the law had not said, 'You shall not covet.'" In other words, the law is necessary. It exposes our mess, the mess of every single one of us. It proves that "none is righteous, no, not one."[4] And that "all have sinned and fall short of the glory of God."[5] It declares us guilty and sentences us to death. It is not until we have experienced death that we will see the need for a new life.

There is simply nothing that we can do to be born again.[6] The law condemns and Christ makes alive. The law serves us death so that Christ can restore us to a new life of union with him and create a new identity as the Beloved.

Author and Old Testament scholar Chad Bird writes,

> The way [Christ] deals with you is not by catering to your every desire, spoiling you by giving you whatever your heart craves. That is not the way of our Lord. The way in which He deals with His church, the way He deals with all of you, is by killing you—killing you so that, having been put to death, you might truly live in Him. The way He deals with you is by making you nothing—nothing so that He might recreate you to be everything that He is: holy, righteous, and blameless in the eyes of Our Father in heaven.[7]

The law kills by tearing down every possible belief that we can do life on our own. It kills all self-effort to maintain who it is that we think we are or need to be. It puts to death our false notions of believing that we are doing a good job at being holy in our own efforts. It shows us who we really are without Jesus: liars, cheaters, adulterers, murderers, idolaters, and the like.

> That is what we are, plain and simple: a league of the guilty. But don't despair— the good news is yet to come.

The law strips off the fig leaves that we shamefully try to hide behind so that the gospel can come in and clothe us in the righteousness of Christ. Just like a sweater of self-approval that gets unraveled, leaving us naked, we must first be undressed before we can be clothed. So it is in this way that we can see how God allows the law to expose us so that we may see the sweetness of the gospel all the more.

Francis Spufford, author of *Unapologetic*, speaks the truth about Christianity when he says,

> Christianity isn't supposed to be about gathering up the good people (shiny! happy! squeaky clean!) and excluding the bad people (frightening! alien! repulsive!) for the very simple reason that there aren't any good people. . . . [Christianity] certainly can slip into being a club or a cozy affinity group or a wall against the world. But it isn't supposed to be. What it's supposed to be is a league of the guilty.[8]

That is what we are, plain and simple: a league of the guilty. But don't despair—the good news is yet to come.

FOR THE JOURNEY

1. In what ways do you find it hard to admit your messiness? How does the culture of the church you are in help or hinder you in being vulnerable with others?

2. What does the law reveal about us?

3. Why is it important to understand the role of the law? How does that distinction affect you in your daily life?

The Imposter, Myself, and I

The reason we aren't honest is that we are playing a game called let-me-show-you-that-I'm-a-good-Christian and the game is killing a lot of Christians who have left the fellowship because they simply couldn't play the game anymore.

Steve Brown

And so, like runaway slaves, we either flee our own reality or manufacture a false self which is mostly admirable, mildly prepossessing, and superficially happy. . . . We hide behind pretty faces which we put on for the benefit of our public. And in time we may even come to forget that we are hiding, and think that our assumed pretty face is what we really look like.

Simon Tugwell

It is better to live naked in the truth than clothed in fantasy.

Brennan Manning

From the outside looking in, my life hardly looks all that messy. Sure, you might see my kids punching each other at church or catch me rolling my eyes at my husband across the table at the pizza place, but for the most part our family looks and acts pretty put together (at least in public). Sometimes I wonder if I am even the one who should be writing a book on being a mess (that is, until I read back through chapter 1!).

I like to think I'm doing okay these days. But really, that's just another part of my mess—the part that I hide behind to make you think that I *am* okay. The part that shoves aside anything that might not look pretty to others, hoping it will evaporate and not ever need to be dealt with. It's my imposter. It's who I am when I forget the goodness of what Christ has done.

You see, I'm like a duck. I may appear to be gliding across the water gracefully as the cares of life roll off my back, but when you look beneath the surface, you can see my webbed feet paddling wildly, creating bubbles and turmoil under the water. The fact that I look good from the top doesn't mean that I'm not frantic underneath. I love to make my exterior look good. I love to hide behind whatever I can come up with on any given day to make myself appear to be put together. I love to play pretend. I love to hide my messiness.

Maybe you are like me. Or maybe you are more like a duck swimming upside down on its back; your mess is faceup for the world to see, too shambolic to be suppressed under the water. Either way, we are the same; both furiously kicking at the shame that threatens to drown us.

My imposter is the part of me that has spent years building an identity worthy of other people's approval. I began to fashion her in a dark, empty corner of my mind as a little girl. And as I grew and my mind filled up with greater things, leaving no more room for her to hide, she was eventually pushed out into full view. There was no more suppressing her. She learned to love accolades and approval, and she became an accomplished athlete for the sake of acceptance: acceptance from herself, and acceptance from those around her. She learned that performance was everything, and with that she knew just the right things to do and not do to gain favor with those around her.

My imposter has changed with each season of my life. She has been the athletic performance-driven people pleaser, the rule-keeping good girl, and the "I-can-do-it-all-and-do-it-well" supermom. These days I find her maturing and becoming much more refined in the ways that she makes herself present. I have relied heavily on her performance, and each time she fails I find that she sweeps her failure under the rug, hoping nobody will notice, molding herself into whatever is next on the list; whatever suits the world that I am living in at the present moment. The imposter in me longs to speak eloquently and to have all the right answers. She longs to come across as intelligent and put together. My imposter desires kudos. She does everything she can to hide her weaknesses and showcase her strengths. She longs more than anything to impress you.

Because my imposter *is* what she *does,* she is terrified of exposure. And rightly so! Exposure is painful. It forces us to confront our imposter, convince her of her sin, and be kind enough to deliver her to the feet of Jesus.

We Fear Exposure

A wise friend once told me, "The real flavor of a tea bag comes out in hot water." There is amazing truth in his statement. I've seen this manifested in many ugly ways, in others and in me. We do not yet know what our hearts are truly hanging on to until we have been exposed. This is why we run from conflict, cover up our sin, and justify our poor behavior. We would rather work ourselves to death to hide the truth than undergo the painful and humiliating experience of allowing the truth to come out.

That's certainly the case for me. While I have revealed much of my mess to you, I'm still not who you think I am. Heck, I'm not even who *I* think I am. I've only shared with you what I've chosen to share with you. I've only told you the stuff that makes me look broken enough. The truth is that my propensity is always to cover up my natural, raw self. I don't think we could handle complete exposure of the brokenness of every human being. Only God can see it all.

There will always be more to the story. As human beings, and Christians in particular, we fear exposure. We fear being found out. "The false self is skilled at the controlled openness that scrupulously avoids any significant self-disclosure."[1]

My imposter, my false self, has become quite proficient at keeping me from fully exposing my mess. Perhaps it's because I have believed the lie that full exposure leads only to shame and destruction. And so I have worked hard to release to those around me just the right information in just the right way to show you that I am being honest, all the while hiding what might fully expose me for who I really am. Self-protection does not allow me to fully disclose to you how bad I really am. I fear your judgment. I fear your wrath. I fear the loss of your approval. And so I tell you just enough. I tell you 99 percent of my failure. Sometimes I am aware of what I am doing, and at other times I don't even realize the lying of my own heart because it has me deceived as well. After all, "The heart is deceitful above all things, and desperately sick; who can understand it?" (Jer. 17:9).

There are still many things in my heart that have yet to bubble over. If I knew everything in there, I wouldn't be so surprised at my reaction to that hateful email I just got. I wouldn't be struggling with pride as I read and reread that flattering text. There's more in this heart, so much more. It has settled at the bottom and needs only to be stirred a little for it to come to the surface.

I often approach God with the same fear of judgment and wrath that I worry about from the people around me. I try my best to hide from him, yet he always pulls the curtain back on my heart. It seems ridiculous that I would do this over and over again only to be found and loved. Perhaps I just like a good game of hide-and-seek.

The Skins We Wear

Although I may be the most transparent person you know, I am only picking and choosing what it is that I want to reveal to you and how vulnerable I am really going to allow myself to be. At times I find myself moving from one kind of imposter to another, simply out of self-protection.

My boys, like most boys their ages, have a crazy obsession with a video game called Minecraft. In the game you have an avatar (the character you choose to represent yourself), and you are able to choose the way your avatar looks. My boys work hard to save their money to buy different "skins" for their avatars so that they can change their appearance. Some days they might be a skeleton while other days they might look like the Incredible Hulk; the possibilities are vast and wide.

In today's age of social media, it is all too easy to be someone else, to change the skins of our imposters. We are able to daily fashion ourselves into anything we want others to think we are, endlessly hiding from our regret by becoming who we wish we could actually be. Actor Woody Allen once said, "My one regret in life is that I am not someone else."[2] How true this rings for most of us, at least those of us who are brave enough to be honest.

Just like my sons change the appearance of their avatars, I also change skins on a regular basis. I had an awakening to this as some friends came to our house for the first time. On social media I am known for posting about some of the craziness that happens in our home with the hashtag #embracethechaos. It's my way of getting through the day, making fun of what could really make me mad if I didn't laugh at it. And to be honest, I enjoy the reaction I get from others. Though I don't believe I have exaggerated the truth about my family, I have chosen to share only those things that happen that are utterly ridiculous and humorous. It would be lame if I tweeted about getting the laundry done . . . again. Or about the healthy dinner we just ate. So I tend to share the extreme stuff. And therefore the world that is looking on from a distance believes that life in our home is always extreme. Some are exhausted by it, others entertained, and some might even be jealous, wishing that they could see their family through the lens of humor that I pretend frames mine.

In any case, this was all revealed to me in one simple statement from a friend's husband, who had never been to our home. As he walked through the door his first words to me were, "Your house isn't at all as bad as what you make it out to be on Facebook!" Now mind you, I did not spend hours cleaning my house to impress him. I had just spent hours babysitting my friend's four kids, which meant eight children in the house under the age of ten. It meant that dress-up clothes, LEGOs, dishes, sticks, rocks, toy guns, puzzles, and anything else you can think of had been pulled from the deep recesses of our closets and from underneath our beds. The truth is, I feel safe hiding behind a fabricated version of myself, my "skin" of the day.

I am not the only one who has fashioned an imposter-self to hide behind. We have all done it. I think that if you thought long and hard enough about it, you would agree that you do the very same thing. Some of this is a conscious effort to cover up. It stems from our belief that Christians aren't supposed to be messy, that Christians are supposed to have it all together and be shiny, happy people for the glory of God. And so we work feverishly to hide our mess. We think that if we can just give others 99 percent of our real failure, then we are okay—even those of us who preach that we need to be real. We make light of failure by announcing on Facebook how our recent recipe was a "fail" or the fact that we committed a major "mom fail" by being late to pick up our kids from school. It's all just a nice little cover-up for the real messes we are. We don't share about the lustful thoughts we've had that day or how we bullied our son last night. I've never seen a Facebook status that announced, "I yelled at my kids, ignored my spouse, and then watched some porn while I drank a whole bottle of wine." That's too much! The last thing we want is for the world to know what flavor our tea is!

> I've never seen a Facebook status that announced, "I yelled at my kids, ignored my spouse, and then watched some porn while I drank a whole bottle of wine." That's too much! The last thing we want is for the world to know what flavor our tea is!

Though our motivations may differ, the reality is that since the garden we have all been hoarding skins with our allowance and changing them as our mood fits.

We know that we aren't perfect, and so we try to cover our shame with a cleaned-up version of ourselves, or sometimes a more humorous version of ourselves. Whatever it is that we think will make us acceptable to the outside world, ourselves, and God, we have a skin for it. Skin swapping happens when we change how we look, how we act, or what we seem to care about for the sake of making ourselves look better than we actually are. I can be "Hannah Homemaker," "Rodeo Rita," or "Barbara the Bookworm" all in the course of a few short hours depending on who I am talking to that day. We are quite skilled at the craftiness it takes to design and execute an imposturous self, often without realizing we have stepped out of one skin and right into another.

Since the first time we sensed someone's disappointment with us we began building the layers, creating skins that depict the person we long to be, think we should be, or want others to think we are. Your imposter is not the same as my imposter. Perhaps you learned early on that the negative attention you received as a rebel was better than no attention at all, and so you continued to act out, labeling yourself as hardcore, hoping that nobody would really know how scared you were on the inside. Maybe you have crafted a kind of renegade costume that you wear in front of others, pretending not to care about consequences, yet you are haunted by the guilt when all is quiet and you lie awake in the darkness of your lonely room.

Or maybe you have created the image of a person who has it all together, one whom others look up to—yet it's just a holier-than-thou mask to cover your inner mess. While our imposters are not our true selves, it's hard for us to recognize the lie that we have been living. We so easily don our imposters' skins that we no longer notice when we're putting them on. And when it is pointed out we passionately deny it because of our fear of being exposed for who we really are.

The Imposter Factory

Sadly, the church has played a large role as a breeding ground for imposters. Many congregations have become nothing more than imposter factories, preaching to grace-starved sinners the bad news that they must find a way to clean themselves up in order to fit in. And if we are brave enough to take off our fig leaves and show our mess to other Christ followers, we are often confronted with tips and tricks (with ascribed Scripture) to help clean us up. Self-help books line the shelves of bookstores, telling us how to get our acts together and promising that if we follow their prescriptions we will be transformed into "new and better" selves and have the victorious Christian lives we've always dreamed of.

When the law is twisted into something that we must *do*, it causes us to go into imposter mode all the more. When the church tells us that we can't be messy, we either run and say, "To hell with you and your God," or we stick around and stuff our mess into our back pocket as we walk through the door to teach Sunday school.

We confuse the law with the gospel, thinking that if we can just follow the law it will save us. This confusion pushes us into the manufacturing efforts of the imposter-self. When we are told that we aren't good enough (because the law says that we aren't), our natural inclination is either to say, "I'm out of here" or to get busy fashioning a self that we think *is* good enough. We often believe we are getting along quite well when we are really just hiding behind the false self that we have manufactured. The law without the gospel drives us to pride or to despair; it manipulates us into believing either that we can do something about our desperation by merely trying harder or that we're hopeless. Those who stick around are left with nothing but a bootstrap theology that tells them that it's up to them to prove their worthiness.

> We confuse the law with the gospel, thinking that if we can just follow the law it will save us.

No wonder "How to be a better Christian" books sell so well. They are nothing more than manuals for imposter maintenance. We naturally desire something that we can do; we want to lower the bar of the law's out-of-reach standard and make our personal holiness another DIY project to be pinned to our Pinterest board. When you are constantly being told that Christianity is about looking and acting a certain way, you will either be molded into an imprisoned drone or eventually walk away.

I have a good friend whom I have counseled through some difficult and trying circumstances. She and her husband had tried to contact the pastor of their large church many times, asking for help. They called, left cards in the offering basket, and even went down to the office asking to see him. A few of the requests were met with a promise that "somebody" would contact them (nobody did), but mostly the couple was just met with silence.

> When you are constantly being told that Christianity is about looking and acting a certain way, you will either be molded into an imprisoned drone or eventually walk away.

Once I suggested that they find a new church where they could be counseled and supported, the truth came out. The reason why the pastor would not respond is that he will not counsel his congregants. He believes that if you have a life with Jesus, walking obedient to his Word, then you should have no need for counseling.[3] They were told that as Christians they shouldn't have problems. But they did have problems! Big ones! Problems that were only made worse by the guilt and shame that the church was laying on them. They were sinners who needed to know that they were loved, and all they were hearing was that they weren't good enough.

An environment like my friends' church is ripe for imposter breeding. It's a literal imposter factory! Imagine what it would be like to attend a small group in a church where having "problems" was frowned upon. Such communities are basically telling people that Christianity is about knitting yourself a nice little costume to slip into before you head to church. The shame and guilt for being human is enough to kill you. And that is what is happening over and over in many churches today. For some, ending their life is a better option than exposing their mess.

There is simply no tolerance for messy humanity in some circles. I have experienced Bible studies in which sharing real struggles was met with uncomfortable silence while prayers for great-aunt Martha's neighbor's father-in-law's big toe to heal were met with concerned questions and follow-up emails. I once heard a young elder (if that's not an oxymoron I don't know what is) talk of a family who wanted to join the church. He shared that this particular family came with "issues." He treated them as if they were lepers who needed a separate island to worship on. Since the elders at our church were helping me in dealing with some "issues" at that time, I suddenly became ashamed and wondered how the church could tolerate someone like me. My suicide plan was not far behind.

The League of the Pathetic

My family likes to visit a nearby farm. It has a quaint little store where we buy candy and Christmas gifts, and it is also home to a menagerie of donated farm animals that entertain our kids. On a recent visit there I made a profound discovery: the potbelly pig dragged his belly on the ground, the emu acted strangely, the turkey looked as if a lion had taken a bite out of its plume of feathers, and a tiny little rooster, half the size of the hens, appeared to have a short man's complex. Then there was the duck whose wing feathers permanently stuck out to the side, the goat whose oversized belly jiggled as we poked it, and the tortoise who didn't do anything but sit and look pathetic. We began to call them "The League of the Pathetic." It was apparent that these were the reject animals: the ones who were no longer wanted by their owners. The ones not pretty enough for shows or loved enough to stay pets. They were the riffraff of the farms, cast aside because they couldn't live up to someone else's standards.

As I sat and stared at these pitiful beasts and the kids who were so enthusiastically feeding, petting, and talking to them, I saw something beautiful. I saw The League of the Pathetic being loved. I saw kids fighting over who got to pet the giant goat and begging their parents for more corn to stuff him with. I saw kids climbing fences and reaching through the wires to get just one touch of a real-life llama, whose twisted teeth stuck out over his lip. The children passionately desired these animals. The kids didn't care that they were castoffs; they just wanted to be close to them. What began as a spectacle to me became a beautiful picture of the relentless tenderness that Jesus has for his children. Jesus collects the riffraff. He can't wait to be near them. Never once did he require anyone to dress up for him, to pull herself together. He has invited us to come just as we are.

> This is the church that God loves so much. If we are honest, we discover that we are nothing more than a bunch of riffraff with missing feathers, scrunched-up faces, and bellies that drag on the ground. We too are a League of the Pathetic.

This is the church that God loves so much. If we are honest, we discover that we are nothing more than a bunch of riffraff with missing feathers, scrunched-up faces, and bellies that drag on the ground. We too are a League of the Pathetic.[4] And when we fully embrace the gospel we find the freedom to accept our ugliness and our messes as well as those of the people in the pew next to us. This frees us to love each other for who we are and not who we should be. This is where we find Jesus.

The Good News for Imposters

Brennan Manning writes,

> The relentless tenderness of Jesus challenges us to give up our false faces, our petty conceits, our irritating vanities, our preposterous pretending, and become card-carrying members of the messy human community. . . . He invites us into the fellowship of saved sinners wherein our identity and glory lie not in titles, trinkets, honorary degrees, and imaginary differences but in our "new self" in Christ irrevocably bonded to our brothers and sisters in the family of God.[5]

You see, it's not until we finally admit our messiness that we will be able to accept the messes of others. The gospel does just that: it shows us how much we are loved because of Christ, freeing us to believe that we don't have to pretend any longer and that we do not have to expect others to pretend either. When we let others enter into our mess, we give them the much-needed permission to be human themselves.

Yes, our imposters may be pathetic. But imposters are the only ones that God has to work with. He knows our frame.[6] He knows the place where we cry tears of shame. He knows the depth of our woundedness. He knows our sin and our rebellion[7] toward him, yet he chooses to hunt us down and love us. He refuses to let us go. And although we work feverishly to cover up our mess, he is there patiently and lovingly working to expose it so that we may be free.

You may be struggling daily, just as I do, to quiet your imposter. Maybe your daily prayer is that the real you will be free enough to step to the forefront and live as the Beloved. One thing and one thing only will ever free us to step out of our imposter costume, wearing our real skin: knowing our true identity.

Author Nadia Bolz-Weber hits the nail on the head regarding our identity issues when she says,

Identity. It's always God's first move. Before we do anything wrong and before we do anything right, God has named and claimed us as God's own. But almost immediately, other things try to tell us who we are and to whom we belong: capitalism, the weight-loss industrial complex, our parents, kids at school—they all have a go at telling us who we are. But only God can do that. Everything else is temptation. Maybe demons are defined as anything other than God that tries to tell us who we are. And maybe, just moments after Jesus's baptism, when the devil says to him, "If you are the Son of God . . . ," he does so because he knows that Jesus is vulnerable to temptation precisely to the degree that he is insecure about his identity and mistrusts his relationship with God. So if God's first move is to give us our identity, then the devil's first move is to throw that identity into question. Identity is like the tip of a spool of thread, which when pulled can unwind the whole thing.[8]

Under the Robe

For several years my kids were enrolled in a Lutheran school. On the first day of school the kids and parents attended a special chapel service in which the pastor wore his clerical robe and delivered a beautiful gospel message. Each year he used the same illustration, and it is one that I continue to point my kids back to.

He would call up one of the tiny preschoolers, and after he proclaimed the good news of what Christ did for us on the cross, he would ask the kids to imagine that he was Jesus. He would then proceed to hide the preschooler under his garment so that he or she could no longer be seen. With the preschooler no longer in view, the pastor would explain that what the kids were looking at when they saw him in his robe is exactly how God sees his children. We disappear under the robes of Christ's righteousness. Everything that we do from that point forward is done in Christ, hidden by his royal garment, clothed in perfection, and completely justified. Yes, there will be much clumsiness under that long robe, but nothing can cause us to lose its covering. Christ has made us blameless. Christ is now our identity.

Although we are daily plagued by our pathetic imposters who wish to push themselves out from under our robes and make a name for themselves, we can rest assured that they are not our true selves. Our identity is found in who we are in Christ, not what we have fashioned ourselves to be out of fear, greed, pride, and self-righteousness.

In his book *A Traveler Toward the Dawn*, John Eagen speaks of his spiritual director, Bob, who says,

> The heart of it is this: to make The Lord and his immense love for you constitutive of your personal worth. Define yourself radically as one beloved by God. God's love for you and his choice of you constitute your worth. Accept that and let it become the most important thing in your life. . . . Our identity rests in God's relentless tenderness for us revealed in Jesus Christ.[9]

When each of us is reminded of our true worth as one radically loved by God, the imposter is quieted and its power is diminished. Because Christ has secured our identity as his Beloved, we no longer have to yield to the imposter's demands to hide our broken humanity. As we'll see more clearly in the next chapter, we no longer have to live a life in constant fear of being exposed. We can now live in the freedom of knowing that we give glory to God simply by being our ragged, scarred, sorry old selves.

> The good news is that God loves the real version of you, not the cleaned-up, funny, talented, presentable you.

The good news is that God loves the real version of you, not the cleaned-up, funny, talented, presentable you. He loves and relentlessly pursues the wounded, ugly, doubting, struggling-to-get-through-life, belly-dragging-on-the-ground, pathetic you. His love is not conditioned on the fact that you are getting it right. He only calls you to come to him exactly as you are.

FOR THE JOURNEY

1. In what ways might you be hiding behind an imposter?
2. Why is it important to recognize our imposter-selves?
3. How does the law expose our imposter-selves and how does the gospel speak to that exposure?

An Exposure That Leads to Freedom

It is only when a person sees himself to be a genuine sinner with no hope under the Law that the Gospel will be heard as joyous news of pardon.

John T. Pless

The more you see your own flaws and sins, the more precious, electrifying, and amazing God's grace appears to you.

Timothy Keller

The truth will set you free. But not until it is finished with you.

David Foster Wallace

When the law does its job in exposing our sin and pushing our imposter into the light, our sin loses its power over us. Why? Because once the law has exposed our mess and performed its crushing work, it is at that moment that the gospel flies in and we are delivered into the tender hands of Jesus, who promises to deliver us from the shame of our failures. We are free to be wrecked. We are free to be weak. We are free to fail. Having our mess exposed is a painful process, as is every path that leads to freedom, but the reward is sweet.

Just recently God used the writing of this book to expose the deep-seated anger that I have in my heart. For me, writing is very personal. It is how I best see the world. I process life through the *tap, tap, tap* of the keyboard, and I write because I often don't know how I really feel until after I have read what I've written. If I go too long without spilling the words out through my fingers, I feel a pent-up, low-lying rage and want to scratch the nearest person's eyeballs out.

In order to meet the deadline for this book, I planned out exactly how much writing I needed to do per week. I tried to carve out time on the days that my kids were in school and my husband was at work (which after housework and appointments only left me with a few hours a week) so that I could write uninterrupted and without forsaking my first priority as a wife and mother. As I felt the words bubbling up inside of me, I pushed them down, subduing them until my writing day. On one of those days, to limit distractions I had the use of a friend's empty house for as long as I needed. I planned a quiet retreat away from the dishes and laundry and everything else that was demanding my attention at home and that I felt guilty for neglecting. A luxury indeed!

My messenger bag was carefully packed with books and computer and was left by the door so that I could bring it along when I took my daughter to school. After driving thirty minutes into town to drop off my daughter, I realized that I didn't have my bag. Anger and self-pity rushed over me. I scrambled to find a way to make the day work without driving back home to retrieve my things. I called a friend nearby who agreed to let me write on her iPad. It wasn't my ideal choice but it was something.

After a workout at the Y and with borrowed iPad in my hand, I was over the self-pity and ready to get to work. I had three and a half hours of uninterrupted time to pour my heart onto the screen; a heart that had been holding back for weeks, waiting for the floodgates to be opened. But as I drove to the writing sanctuary of my friend's empty house, I realized that I had never texted her for her alarm code so that I could get in. I texted her, I called her, I texted and called her friends to no avail.

I stomped back to my car, cursing in my head, and drove home. I was angry with myself for not planning ahead. I was frustrated with my forgetfulness. But most of all I was angry with God. I had no idea how angry I was until I began to pray. All I could do was curse and blame and tell him that I was finally giving up.

After my long drive of cursing and crying, I arrived home, locked myself in my room (even though there was nobody home),

> The law once again exposed that I was holding on to the belief that God needed my good works. It exposed my false belief that life with God is quid pro quo (a Latin phrase meaning "give something to get something"), and it exposed my unbelief of my belovedness.

and cursed and cried some more. Then I opened my computer and cursed and cried through my fingers. I think it was the nastiest letter I have ever written to anyone, and it was to God! First Corinthians 4:5 tells us that the law will expose the motive of our hearts, and that is just what had happened that morning.

But do you know what? Through my cursing and my crying I began to see the anger that had settled in the bottom of my heart. My frustration wasn't just about not being able to get my work done. It was about so much more. It was about me fighting for control and trusting in myself. It was about fear and approval. The law once again exposed that I was holding on to the belief that God needed my good works. It exposed my false belief that life with God is quid pro quo (a Latin phrase meaning "give something to get something"), and it exposed my unbelief of my belovedness.

The law's exposure of my anger at God led to much repenting behind that locked bedroom door. There was much writing that happened too, as in my anger and repentance my fingers did not stop tapping for two straight hours. Two hours of pouring out my unbelief. Two hours of words that came from a heart that had been exposed by the law. Two hours of confession, repentance, and absolution. God loves me so much that he exposed my heart for what it was. Once again he was showing me that I was his Beloved Mess.

My life is full of exposures like this. I bet yours is too. When we pay attention we begin to see how much of our day is comprised of a string of exposures. Some are just little moments in which the law reveals our ugliness to us, while others are deeply painful collisions of real life and real heartache that leave us wondering if we are going to survive the humiliation of it all.

Talk to anyone whom God has pulled out from the pit of any type of addiction, whether it is drugs, alcohol, porn, self-harm, eating disorders, or even the more acceptable sins of the approval addicts and performance junkies, and they will tell you of the freedom that exposure brought them. The terrifying act of revealing it all that leads to the relief of someone finally knowing those secrets somehow feels so very dangerous yet so very safe at the same time.

The Freedom of Exposure

Rob and Erika's story is a prime example of how the exposure of our sin by the law can lead to freedom. My husband and I had wanted to go out with this couple for a long time. There was something attractive about them. They seemed to ooze a rare freedom not seen in many believers. Their faith was genuine, yet they didn't seem like the typical Christian family. They freely loved those around them with an authentic love and service that didn't seem to be coming from a place of duty or self-righteousness, like many of the other families around us. For this reason I needed to know their story. I knew that there was more. I knew they must have had a major interruption by grace that brought them to this place.

As we sat across the table making small talk, the conversation turned to their upcoming anniversary. When they stated the number of years they had been married, I began to do the math in my head. Their oldest child was the same age. Before I could put two and two together Erika turned to Rob and said, "You might as well tell the whole story." What followed was an absolutely amazing story of grace and freedom. With their permission, I pass their story on to you.

Rob and Erika were both serving in full-time ministry when they met. Rob was on staff with a youth organization and Erika was a missionary living outside of the United States. Their story began with an email from Rob and, a few months later, an adventurous first date.

Rob took several long journeys to visit Erika on the mission field, even joining with her in some of the work that she was doing with orphans there. They quickly fell in love. It wasn't long before the two were engaged and planning for a bright future together in ministry. And then things started to fall apart . . . or so it seemed.

Rob and Erika set aside their deep conviction of waiting for their wedding night to have sex and gave in to the overwhelming power of lust for one another. And this is where their story really begins.

The couple's one slip, their one moment of weakness and compromise, resulted in a life-altering exposure: Erika was pregnant.

With a positive pregnancy test in hand, the only words that she could speak were, "I'm not that girl."

You see, Erika had grown up in a Christian home, attended Christian school, was a faithful youth group participant, became a missionary, and on and on. She had her "résumé of righteousness" all in order and took pride in her outward goodness. In her mind she just wasn't capable of a moral failure such as getting pregnant before her wedding day. Her self-righteousness had her convinced that she would never be *that girl*.

Things did not happen the way Rob and Erika had planned. They didn't plan for their dating life to include sex, and their dream wedding didn't include a baby bump.

Rob and Erika began to work down the list of people whom they felt they needed to tell, starting with their parents. In the end they decided to include a pregnancy announcement with all of their wedding invitations. Hiding the truth would only complicate the situation even further. They had no choice but to embrace their exposure, own up to what they had done, and move forward on the path that God had asked them to walk. All attempts to keep up the appearance of a "good" Christian couple with a pure courtship were no longer necessary. The word of their failure was out. The law had exposed their sin and brought them to their knees begging for grace. It was time for the gospel to come in and heal.

They had nowhere to turn for help but to the Lord, and as they turned to him, they began to see the freedom that God was bringing to them through their exposure. What the young, frightened couple received from their family and friends was more than they could comprehend. From just about everyone they told, they received much love and understanding. When they expected condemnation, they received grace. When they anticipated rejection, they received acceptance. Not every story of exposure ends this way, but theirs did, and it is a beautiful representation of the grace of God.

It was the day that Erika was finally able to utter the words, "I *am* that girl" that Rob and Erika really began to understand how much they were loved by God just as they were. And this is why I enjoy being with them so much. The law had exposed their sin, and the gospel came in and delivered them to freedom. They now understand grace in a way that they never did before, and this has caused them to love Christ and those around them in amazing ways as they minister graciously and patiently to those struggling along the path of life, sometimes even taking them into their home until they are back on their feet.

Once exposed by the law, whether on a smaller scale of heart struggles or major life interruptions, the grace of the gospel is not far behind. Where God uses the law to expose us, he will always offer us grace to heal.

Sweet Healing Grace

In the past year, three close friends of mine have had unfortunate yet needful separations from their husbands. These are all Christian women married to Christian men. All were committed to serving as couples in their churches regularly. I have painstakingly walked with these friends through the arduous circumstances that God has brought them into. Each has a different story, but my counsel has remained the same: You are his Beloved Mess. Most of the time that's all the counsel I have to offer.

While my struggles may be different from theirs, and yours may be different from mine, there is one thing that needs to be agreed upon: we are all big sinners in need of a great Savior. The fact that my marriage is doing well and God has given my husband and me the ability to move forward in grace does not make me any less of a mess than my friends whose marriages are falling apart.

While the tears and the pain of marital dysfunction have invaded the lives of my friends, I have seen one common thread: God's grace has been revealed to them in astounding ways. I believe this is because those who know that they are broken by the law are much closer to the grace of God than those who don't. Had these couples not experienced the pain of having their hearts slashed open and laid bare, they never would have known the sweet healing grace that comes in the midst of the mess.

> Those who know that they are broken by the law are much closer to the grace of God than those who don't.

This is where the gospel flies in to meet us. When the law has done its work in exposing what needs to come into the light and we have been crushed by the weight of our wrongdoing, there is hope. We have something greater than ourselves to look to—the good news of a Savior who came to rescue us from the law and set us free from guilt and shame.

The Gospel Has Wings

When we see how desperate our case is, when the law has exposed us for who we really are and we are crushed in despair, it is then that the gospel flies in to save us. Christ came and lived the law perfectly on our behalf. He followed every rule, loved perfectly, and never once had an impure thought. This is good news! He did it all for you because he knew each and every struggle with sin that you would ever encounter.

Not only did Christ live a flawless life on our behalf, but he then bled on the cross and died the death we deserved, announcing that the fulfillment of the law was finished. He knew the pain of separation from the perfect union with his father so that we would never have to know it. He satisfied *all* of God's wrath for *all* of our sin so that we would gain *all* of his right standing before God and be freed from sin and death. And then he left us with the perfect grace gift of his indisputable record, so that when God looks at us he sees Christ's perfect, impeccable life in place of ours.

Christ became the law-keeper for you and me, the lawbreakers. This, my friends, is great news! God does not despise us in our mess. He is not up in heaven with arms crossed, waiting for us to get our act together. Rather, he is working in the midst of our mess to show us how much he really does love us as we are. He delights in showing us mercy and grace. Every mess of ours that the law exposes is used in some way or another to show his magnificence. Nothing is wasted.

> When we stop stuffing down and hiding our failures, we see that God really does love us just as we are. This is freedom! We are no longer enslaved to our shortcomings. We no longer have to hide in shame.

No matter what kind of mess the law has revealed, we can rest knowing that "the Gospel contains no demand, only the gift of God's grace and truth in Christ. It has nothing to say about works of human achievement and everything to say about the mercy of God for sinners."[1]

You see, the issue is not whether we are a mess, because the law proves that we all are. But because the law no longer has dominion over us, we are finally free to admit that we are a mess. And when we stop stuffing down and hiding our failures, we see that God really does love us just as we are. This is freedom! We are no longer enslaved to our shortcomings. We no longer have to hide in shame.

As we saw in Rob and Erika's story, when the law does its job in exposing our sin and pushing us into the light, our sin loses its power over us and we begin to experience the freedom that Christ died for.

Blogger Lauren Larkin writes,

> The law works for, serves the Gospel, so that exposure is exposure into the light. . . . Into your exposure enters this God, into your dirt and crap and unjustness and fleshiness walks this good, good, God. And He's unafraid to touch you, to grab you in his strong arms and carry you into real life. Repeatedly. It's not a one-time thing. We are repeatedly exposed and repeatedly loved—minute to minute, hour to hour, day to day, week to week, month to month, and year to year. His mercies are new *every* morning . . . every morning dawn that follows the dusk of our sin.[2]

I have seen this time and again in my own life when I feel stuck in the self-condemnation of my secret sins. My burden is alleviated when I tell a trusted friend. When we speak our fears, shame, and confusion over our failures out loud, we begin to see that we are not alone and the prison that we have placed ourselves in has suddenly vanished.

> When we believe, and I mean actually believe, not just confess, that the cross was about us and our sin and our failure, there is no reason left for us to hide.

When we believe, and I mean actually believe, not just confess, that the cross was about us and our sin and our failure, there is no reason left for us to hide. We no longer have to fear exposure. The law exposes us all for the mess that we are. After all, "None is righteous, no, not one" (Rom. 3:10). Knowing this gives us the ability to stop pretending that we really *aren't* that bad. The shame and the makeup and the walls and the masks—they all come crumbling down when the gospel enters in. The beauty of the cross is that we no longer have to look to ourselves and our performance for "good news." We no longer have to hide behind our proverbial fig leaf. It's been ripped away. At the cross God's love for us held his Son there, fully exposed, having become sin for us that we may have freedom through his righteousness given to us.

If you are in Christ, there is not one ounce of judgment left for you. Not one drop of wrath left in the cup. It is finished. You are free to be exposed to the fullest. Like Rob and Erika, like me, you no longer have any reason to hide. In fact, you can embrace your exposure by the law, knowing that the clearest, most magnificent views of grace come from our ugliest, most horrifying exposures.

FOR THE JOURNEY

1. In what way has the law exposed you, leaving you desperate for the good news of the gospel?
2. Have you ever had a moment of exposure that has led you into freedom? How did the gospel come in and free you?
3. What are some of the ways that the law exposes your heart daily? How does the gospel speak to each one of these little or big exposures?

Romans 8:1 on Repeat

With the arrival of Jesus, the Messiah, that fateful dilemma is resolved. Those who enter into Christ's being-here-for-us no longer have to live under a continuous, low-lying black cloud. A new power is in operation. The Spirit of life in Christ, like a strong wind, has magnificently cleared the air, freeing you from a fated lifetime of brutal tyranny at the hands of sin and death.

Romans 8:1–2, Message

> Feelings come and feelings go,
> And feelings are deceiving;
> My warrant is the Word of God—
> Naught else is worth believing.
>
> Though all my heart should feel condemned
> For want of some sweet token,
> There is One greater than my heart
> Whose Word cannot be broken.

I'll trust in God's unchanging Word
Till soul and body sever,
For, though all things shall pass away,
His Word shall stand forever!

Martin Luther

As a mom, I have a keen sense of when an argument is about to break out among my kids. I am often able to step into the room and redirect the conversation before the room becomes a bloody battleground. However, as my kids get older it seems that their desire to be right and to make sure others know that they are right is growing stronger than any rebuke from Mom.

One particular morning when friends were visiting, I overheard the "nuh-uhs" starting and I began to make my way from the back of the house to intervene. Only this time, instead of jumping in, I stopped and listened to what they were discussing. One of their friends had made the innocent, yet theologically inaccurate, statement that "only good people go to heaven." My kids just couldn't hold back. I believe it was my then eight-year-old who said, "Nuh-uh. Getting to heaven isn't about being good enough. Even murderers can go to heaven if they have Jesus."

This gospel momma could not have been more proud. While I don't teach my kids to go around and hunt out bad theology in third graders, I am definitely militant on teaching them the gospel, and sometimes it comes out in humorous, immature ways. For some reason the "murderers go to heaven" line is my kids' favorite, and I've heard them use it several times. (No, I'm not afraid that my kids will grow up to be murderers because they believe this.)

What if I told you that right now, no matter what you have just done, if you are in Christ, you stand uncondemned? You are acceptable before God. There is not one ounce of judgment from God left for you in this life. No matter what you do, you remain safe within the gates of grace. You are secure, and there is nothing that you can do to lose that.

I don't know about you, but this sounds like crazy talk to me! Really? If I commit some vile, heinous crime, God will not condemn me if I am in Christ? How is that even possible?

Aren't there earthly consequences for such sins? Of course! Horrible, awful things come from such acts. There should be consequences. There should be retribution. There will be punishment. I'm not saying to go out and commit such acts. I am simply saying that even the worst sin we can think of is, for the believer, covered by Christ's blood.

I have no hesitation in preaching freedom to you. I don't believe that the message of grace will make you go off the deep end. I don't need your permission to sin, nor do you need mine.

Grace offends us. It is an uncomfortable thought to believe that once Christ has saved us there is nothing, and I mean *absolutely nothing*, we can do to step outside of his grace. We like our to-do lists; we like to think that we are doing good things so that we can make God love us so he will keep us in his club. We fear that if we tell others (especially the really messy others) that they are loved no matter what, they won't obey God. Or that they will dive headfirst into debauchery, and maybe tell other people that God loves them just as they are.

> Grace offends us. It is an uncomfortable thought to believe that once Christ has saved us there is nothing, and I mean **absolutely nothing**, we can do to step outside of his grace.

One young woman even shared with me that for her entire life, her family has gone so far as to tell her that if she embraces the message of grace and freedom, she will become a harlot or a drunkard. She has yet to find freedom in "living under the banner of 'it is finished'"[1] out of fear of being shunned by her family. She lives in constant fear of their condemnation.

I can so relate, but the condemnation I suffer comes from within, not without. I struggle to live within my belovedness that tells me I am free, and I often beat myself up for that which has already been paid for.

The List

During my early thirties, my overactive guilt glands were at their peak, and introspection was killing me. For several years, every day felt like a matter of survival. Every day felt like failure.

Among my drawer full of books that instructed me on how to be a better Christian, wife, mother, etc., was a list that I had made that I would add to often. It was a list of my sins. A list that grew longer by the minute. A list that I had made so that I could try to make things right. I would work hard during the day to right my wrongs or try to do good deeds that might cancel them out, but it didn't alleviate the guilt. Every night I would pull it out, stare down at it and wonder how I could ever be forgiven for all that I had done, let alone be loved by anyone who knew this about me. I thought I had to pay God back and was desperate for something tangible that I could do to make things right. The list became an obsession, to the point that I could feel its presence in that drawer throughout the day. It was calling out to me the shame of the secrets from which I longed to be set free.

While the sins on that list were all valid, it wasn't the exhaustive list that it should have been. The truth is that I had broken far more of God's laws than that list represented. It was ridiculous to think that I could account for them all. During the period of my life when I kept this list, I knew very little of God's grace. I had spent my entire Christian life hearing and believing that the gospel was what we preached to nonbelievers so that they would believe and be saved. I believed that since I was a Christian it was up to me to stay in God's good graces until the very end. I did not understand that because of Christ, there was nothing that I could do to be separated from God's love. In my mind what was on that list was exactly what separated me from the love of God. I could not stand the guilt of my failures. The list was killing me.

I started seeing a counselor for my depression, and after several months I confessed to her that I had this list. To my horror my counselor asked me to bring it to her. With much trepidation, I pulled it from my pocket in our next meeting and laid it out on the table. There it was, *The List*—everything that I never wanted anyone to know about me—laid out in the open, and I was laid out in utter vulnerability. I could not think of a more humiliating experience.

Without reading the list, my counselor handed me a permanent marker and instructed me to write "PAID!" across the words that I had felt so much shame and guilt about. She told me of everything Jesus had done in order to destroy the list I had kept. She told me of the freedom that comes with having a debt paid off. And how all of the sins on my list, every one, had been laid upon Jesus's back and died with him in his death, and that my sins were "cast into the sea of God's forgotten memory."[2] And then she shared Psalm 103:10–13 (NLT):

> He does not punish us for all our sins
>> he does not deal harshly with us, as we deserve.
> For his unfailing love toward those who fear him
>> is as great as the height of the heavens above the earth.
> He has removed our sins as far from us
>> as the east is from the west.
> The Lord is like a father to his children,
>> tender and compassionate to those who fear him.

Imprisoned by Guilt

If only we could really, truly grasp hold of this truth! Far too many of us have believed for far too long that we stand condemned, that God is mad at and disgusted with us.

When I forget the truth that there is no condemnation for me, I wallow in my sin and treat guilt as an idol. I hold on to my guilt by replaying my sin over and over in my head. I simply cannot let it go. Guilt imprisons me.

Perhaps, as I did, you balk at the idea of guilt being an idol. When I first encountered this, I mulled it over for quite a bit. I fought against the idea. How could one possibly make guilt into an idol? Isn't guilt an indication that you have done something wrong? And isn't that a good thing? When I hear the word *idol*, I hear an angry preacher yelling at me to turn away from the bad things that take us away from God. But in reality idols aren't necessarily bad things in and of themselves. We create an idol out of something when we take a good thing and make it an ultimate thing. So all in all I *am* right when I say that guilt is a good thing. Guilt is the red flag of my conscience that convicts my heart. However, I make guilt an idol when I set it up on a pedestal so that I can focus on it and beat myself up, believing that it is up to me to rid myself of that guilt—something that is impossible for me to do on my own.

Rather than live in the freedom and spaciousness of forgiveness, we live imprisoned by self-condemnation. We focus on our failures, which leads us to build our own guilt prisons, lock the door, and toss the key just far enough out of reach to taunt us as we long for freedom but can't seem to grasp it.

Probably none of us have ever built ourselves a physical prison, but we often build hypothetical prisons, condemning ourselves for what has already been forgiven. More often than not, we manufacture prisons in our minds and lock ourselves in, not allowing ourselves to live in the freedom that God longs for us to enjoy. We think that grace is too good to be true, so we shun God's words of freedom and bind ourselves to the law that the gospel has already set us free from.

When we live this way, we are constantly being shut up in a prison of guilt, whether by our own consciences or by well-meaning Christians who believe that if they can just motivate us enough, we will change. It's as if we are being told to just reach out and grab what is ours but God keeps cruelly snatching it away. As author Paul Zahl says, "For fear to end, guilt must end. For guilt to end, atonement must be made. For this to happen, God alone can be responsible."[3] In order for us to break free from the prison of guilt, we must understand that there is no possible way that we can fulfill the law in thought, word, and deed.

None.

Many preachers and teachers are softening the blow of the law by teaching tips and tricks on how to be a better Christian (which only brings about legal-ism) when what we really need is to hold the law in higher regard. A high view of the law frees imprisoned, burdened believers to live a life overflowing with thankfulness for Christ's finished work on their behalf.

> I make guilt an idol when I set it up on a pedestal so that I can focus on it and beat myself up, believing that it is up to me to rid myself of that guilt—something that is impossible for me to do on my own.

The truth is, it's hard work to believe that there is nothing left for us to do. And so by default our hearts freak out when the prison door is opened. We've grown accustomed to life there. We've unpacked the boxes and hung the pictures on the wall. We don't always know what to do with the freedom, and we are slow to leave the cell. We want to grab hold of the bars, take something, anything, with us that gives us comfort, not because it is good for us but simply because it's what we've always known. And so we begin to fashion idols that make us feel safe and in control.

We believe that if we can just get it right, if we can just be good enough, then we will finally be able to rest in the comforting words of Romans 8:1. But what our stubborn, law-laden hearts refuse to believe is that this verse is for people who keep screwing up. We like to skip over the end of Romans 7 where Paul tells of his present-tense mess, his struggle with obedience, and his realization that he is much worse than he can possibly imagine.

> The truth is, it's hard work to believe that there is nothing left for us to do. And so by default our hearts freak out when the prison door is opened.

I have discovered this principle of life—that when I want to do what is right, I inevitably do what is wrong. I love God's law with all my heart. But there is another power within me that is at war with my mind. This power makes me a slave to the sin that is still within me. Oh, what a miserable person I am! Who will free me from this life that is dominated by sin and death? Thank God! The answer is in Jesus Christ our Lord. So you see how it is: In my mind I really want to obey God's law, but because of my sinful nature I am a slave to sin. (vv. 21–25 NLT)

Along with Paul, I struggle with doing what I know is right. I find life in this body incredibly frustrating and often fall into despair over my own wrongdoing. I can go on and on about how every time I try to do something good I end up failing. This is exactly what happens whenever we stop at Romans 7 and leave Jesus out of the picture. Like Paul we must move past the despair and self-pity and into the beautiful truths of what Christ has done for us.

All Day, Every Day

When we agree with Paul that we too are the chief of sinners (1 Tim. 1:15), then we will see just how sweet these words really are:

There is therefore now no condemnation for those who are in Christ Jesus. (Rom. 8:1)

The Christian life is Romans 8:1 on repeat. Because the law that is written on our hearts is constantly telling us that we are the chief of sinners, we must hear all day every day that we are not condemned.

To better understand how we live uncondemned, how our guilt has been removed, consider the process of stain removal. As you likely know, the process of stain removal is not so much about the stain disappearing as it is about transferring the stain from the soiled garment to the clean cloth. It is suggested that you use a white cloth as the blotting rag. This way, when blotting the stain with the rag soaked in stain-removing solvent, you will begin to see the stain transfer onto the white rag. There is an exchange that happens between the two pieces of material. The dirty one begins to come clean as the stain is transferred over to the clean white blotting rag. What once was dirty has become clean because what once was clean took the stain onto itself. Grace is the solvent that allows the stain to be lifted.

> Grace is the solvent that allows the stain to be lifted.

Something similar happens to the believer. Just as the once-dirty garment is now clean because of the transfer, so are we clean because of Christ. Christ blots out our transgressions, taking the stain on himself and making us clean. And even better than that, he now clothes us in unstainable clothes. Nothing sticks. "I, I am he who blots out your transgressions for my own sake, and I will not remember your sins" (Isa. 43:25).

Your stain has been removed! Not only that, but there has been a transfer of your badness for his goodness. Your sins have been blotted out and are remembered no more.

The Day Grace Broke Through

I'd like to say that the day my counselor made me write "PAID" across my list of sins, I was forever free from my prison of guilt. But that is not the case. In fact, I felt angry. I was insulted that there was nothing *I* could do to make up for all of the awful things *I* had done. I was offended by this gospel that she so adamantly preached to me week after week. I told myself one day that if she brought up the gospel one more time, I was going to get up and walk out of the office. Of course she did, and of course I didn't get up and leave. The Holy Spirit glued me to that seat. I could not escape his furious longing for me to hear the truth.

I believe that this was the day that the message of grace finally broke through my hardened pharisaical heart, and I began to believe that I could rest in my forgiveness. It was then that I began to grasp hold of the comforting truth that "God's love never shudders at the state we're in."[4] He was not disgusted with me. As Francis Spufford so beautifully notes,

> He is never disgusted. He never says that anything—anyone—is too dirty to be touched. That anyone is too lost to be found. Wreckage may be written into the logic of the world, but he will not agree that it is all there is. He says, more can be mended than you fear. Far more can be mended than you know.[5]

If you are in Christ, there is no condemnation for you. Not now, not ever. Let these words rest on your heart and settle in your bones. Believe that you really are free. Believe that you really are loved as you are, mess and all.

FOR THE JOURNEY

1. Why do you think it is so difficult for many of us to believe that even the worst sin that we can think of could be forgiven by God?
2. How does this change your view of condemnation within the confines of the relationship between God and man?
3. In what ways is guilt an idol in your life? Or is it?
4. How does the law speak to our guilt, and how does the gospel come in and save us from condemnation?

Stubborn Grace

Grace . . . means that God is pursuing you. That God forgives you. That God sanctifies you. When you are apathetic toward God, He is never apathetic toward you. When you don't desire to pray and talk to God, He never grows tired of talking to you. When you forget to read your Bible and listen to God, He is always listening to you. Grace means that your spirituality is upheld by God's stubborn enjoyment of you. . . . Grace is God's aggressive pursuit of, and stubborn delight in, freakishly foul people.

Preston Sprinkle

What is grace? Grace is love that seeks you out when you have nothing to give in return. Grace is love coming at you that has nothing to do with you. Grace is being loved when you are unlovable. It is being loved when you are the opposite of lovable.

Paul Zahl

I live twenty minutes from the nearest grocery store. Well, that's twenty minutes from any decently sized store with decently priced items. There is the liquor store down the road with the pit bull behind the counter and the largest jugs of Jägermeister you've ever seen. And if the owner likes you as much as he does me, he'll give you his cell number so you can call if you are going to arrive after his 8:00 p.m. closing time and he'll keep the lights on for you. Then there is the market that smells like rotting flesh because of the butcher that occupies the back portion of the building. I'm sure that you can buy amazing carne asada and cow tongue there, but the smell alone keeps me away. And recently a new store has been built nearby where I only stop in for overpriced alcohol and an occasional container of fresh guacamole.

While these stores don't offer the greatest smells, prices, or cleanliness, some of my most liberating moments are found in these hole-in-the-wall places. There's something freeing about being able to show up with no makeup on and my unwashed hair shoved under a hat, wearing my worst pair of cutoffs and my husband's T-shirt that I slept in the night before, to snag a six-pack of beer, some cheap wine, a bag of chips, and fresh guacamole.

I feel free because there's no explanation needed. There's no question as to whether I'm doing it right or not; in fact, I'm *expected* to show up to the liquor store messy. After all, the best customers are the really messy ones.

Although I talk a lot about my messiness, I still have a hard time believing that I am all that messy; that I'm no better than the other liquor store patrons. I like to believe that I'm a respectable Christian woman who is doing all the right things to keep her amazing family respectable. But I'm not. That's why I feel free in the liquor store. The problem is that I've learned to play the game. I've learned to hide my mess and pretend I am okay.

While I may not be an alcoholic, I have just as much of an addiction. I have an addiction to self-approval—an addiction that God has been gently dealing with while I write this book. What you are reading is a result of not only past struggles but also the very real and recent present-tense anguishes of my messy heart.

End of My Rope

In the summer of 2014, soon after I signed the contract to write this book, depression overcame me and threw its wet woolen blanket over me once again, tackling me to the ground. I was stuck, unable to move forward no matter how much effort I mustered. What I thought was a part of my past story had suddenly and terrifyingly become part of the present one. Shame stood at the foot of my bed, ready to walk with me throughout my days, while fear slept alongside of me, whispering lies into my ear by night.

The despair I felt was unbearable. I turned to everything possible to make the pain go away, only to find that I simply could not escape it.

God gave me a precious friend who was faithful to hold my arms up, as Aaron did for Moses, during this time of weak knees and little faith. She helped me to keep moving forward. She reminded me over and over again that I am his Beloved Mess and so is she. She told me that although I felt hopeless, I needed to keep doing the "next thing" so that I didn't add to my hopelessness. She stubbornly proclaimed to me that God was not mad at me, whether I believed that or not. And she assured me that his grip was tight, his grace was sustaining me, and I was going to be okay.

I struggled to make sense of the pain. Like anyone who is faced with a difficult season, I wanted to know why I was going through this. It was when I finally stopped trying to fix myself and accepted the reality of the state I was in that God gently began to reveal to me once again that he doesn't love me for what I can do for him; he loves me for the mess that I am.

One of the ways that he stubbornly showed me this was through a song called *Undone* by Weezer. I suddenly heard my own voice speaking to God through the chorus that says, "If you want to destroy my sweater / Hold this thread as I walk away / Watch me unravel . . ."[1]

God is in the business of sweater destruction. His love for me is so deep that he would not allow me to continue to find my worth in what I did for him, which is ironically the very thing that I preach against. The sweater of self-approval that I had painstakingly knitted over the years had once again been unraveled. It was time for me to start believing the message I was so faithfully distributing to everyone else. It was time to stop covering myself and truly believe that I was his Beloved Mess.

God was my thread-holder as I walked away (and sometimes ran), and my sweater unraveled, leaving me lying on the floor naked and undone. (Actually it had me lying in my bed, eating guacamole, drinking cheap wine, and shamelessly watching episodes of *Desperate Housewives* or some other ridiculous show, which I think you would agree is just as despairing.)

One of the most influential books I read during this time was Mike Yaconelli's *Messy Spirituality*. On a particularly difficult night when I could not see past my sin and despair and find any hope that God could love a loser like me, my faithful friend, knowing how deeply Mike Yaconelli's book had resonated with me, read these words to me over the phone.

> Buried in the back of my mind is the gnawing worry that my grace credit card is going to be cancelled. Parked somewhere in my subconscious is the belief that grace and forgiveness are lavish, unconditional, and *limited*.

Cross Jesus one too many times, fail too often, sin too much, and God will decide to take his love back. . . . Nothing can stop God from loving us. Nothing. He just keeps loving us. He loves us when we don't want him to. He loves us when we don't act like a Christian. He loves us when our lives are a mess. His love is sticky, resistant to rejection, aggressive, and persistent. The challenge is on, so go ahead—resist his love, run from it, hide from it. Go ahead and try.[2]

I was certain that I had gone too far. I had treated my family unfairly because of my pain. I had given up on the idea that God could love me even when I was lashing out at the world around me. I wasn't necessarily depressed because of my sin, but my response to my depression had certainly inflamed my already sinful heart. I couldn't see an end to the pain and destruction that I was causing. I believed that I had crossed the line of grace (there is no such line, by the way), and the only hope I had was to give in to the lie that my family would be better off without me. But what I began to see in the following weeks was that I had once again come to the end of myself.

I've heard it said that God's office is at the end of our rope. And my rope, as frayed and jacked up as it was, had slipped from my hands, dropping me onto God's desk. Not to be lectured, not to have a performance review, but to be thrown into the arms of the almighty Savior, whether I wanted to be or not.

Grace is best discovered when we are at our breaking point. It's hard to see our need for Jesus when we are attempting—in vain—to fulfill that need ourselves. And I was doing exactly that. Or at least I thought I was. But God loves me too much to let me wear that ugly sweater for long. The revealing of the ugliness of my heart had made it impossible for me to continue finding my worth in what I did for God instead of what he has done for me. And although I spent much effort trying to prove that I was an exception, a case too difficult for him to handle, he stubbornly stuck with me. That's grace.

Grace Makes No Exceptions

God's grace for us is not contingent on our performance (Eph. 2:8–9). In fact, Romans 5:20 says, "Where sin increased, grace abounded all the more."

This is good news for the college student who can't face another day with the possibility of failure—the student who has lied to his parents about his grades because he fears their disappointment, and has found himself cheating his way through his final exams. It's good news for the mom who pulls a pocketknife from her purse and slices her leg while sitting in the toy store parking lot, hoping it will relieve the pressure she feels to pull off a nice birthday for her daughter when life seems too bleak to celebrate. It's good news for the man or woman who has once again allowed the allure of the internet to control their life and believed the lie that porn can satisfy their desires and cure their loneliness. It's good news for the woman in the bathroom throwing up her lunch because her weight is the only thing she can control in her life. It's good news for all of us when we believe the lie that any of our sins disqualify us from God's love. It's good news for me as I have been every one of these people in my own way at different times.

> "What? But that doesn't make sense! Christians aren't supposed to struggle with these types of messes. How can you say that God loves people who persist in these kinds of behaviors?" That's the exact lie that I often believe as well. And it's the exact lie that Satan wants us to believe. It's a freedom robber.

Perhaps I have just made you incredibly uncomfortable. Maybe you are saying, "What? But that doesn't make sense! Christians aren't supposed to struggle with these types of messes. How can you say that God loves people who persist in these kinds of behaviors?" That's the exact lie that I often believe as well. And it's the exact lie that Satan wants us to believe. It's a freedom robber.

If you are shocked, if what I've just said enrages your inner law-keeper, if it unnerves you, then good, it should. Grace is shocking, unnerving, and doesn't make sense. I want you to begin to see the stubbornness of grace. Grace refuses to make exceptions, no matter how bad the case.

And now you might be asking, "Is she saying that we are all supposed to go out and embrace our sin so that we may receive more grace?" To paraphrase Paul in Romans 6:1, *Hell no!* Of course that's not what I'm saying! I care very much about the family of God. I care very much about your soul. I grieve deeply over my sin and over the sin of those around me. I *am*, however, acutely aware that we are not just people who occasionally sin, we are *sinners*—people who struggle every day with the reality of failure. When I speak honestly about my struggles I am not promoting my sin nor am I simply too tired to hide it anymore. I am saying what needs to be said. Sharing my failures is not sin endorsement, it's Savior endorsement.

> Grace refuses to make exceptions, no matter how bad the case.

Our Discomfort with Grace

Grace is messy. It is often not given to the person who we think deserves it. Grace doesn't play by the rules. It turns our neat, orderly, religious ideals upside down and shakes out every ounce of security that we might have in our personal rule keeping as well as our judgment of others.

We are uncomfortable with messy. We want people to come in nicely bundled packages, and when they don't, we wonder why they can't just get their act together. Or we take them on as projects hoping to make their messes more tolerable to the church. And because we are uncomfortable with messy, the Christian culture in general is uncomfortable with grace. I wouldn't be preaching real grace if it did not elicit the question that I addressed above. That's what grace does. It causes us to ask questions because it's not as tidy as we think it should be. It seems too good to be true. Grace adopts the absurdly pathetic mess-ups and loves us with an overwhelmingly stubborn love.

> Sharing my failures is not sin endorsement, it's Savior endorsement.

We do not like to be uncomfortable. We want a nice, tame Jesus. We want to keep grace in our pocket. We want to use grace to pacify our Christian efforts, patting ourselves on the back for remembering to show grace to the person who just told us off. Grace refuses to be exploited in this way. An abused grace is not an authentic grace. Grace is not tame. "By God's grace" is not meant to be a nice little tagline for our self-improvement projects. *Grace* is not just a nice word that helps us get through our day; it's the only reason we exist. It's the very air we breathe.

It's this very grace that Christians are missing out on. Since it sounds too good to be true, we pretend that we get it but we don't really believe we do. It comes across in our speech, but our lives don't reflect the radical freedom that living in grace produces.

As author and radio host Steve Brown says, "The church should be a place where we can say anything and know we won't be kicked out, where we can confess our sins knowing others will help us, where we can disagree and still be friends. *It ought to be the one place in the world where we don't have to wear masks.*"³

Churches would be much better off if they were more like my local liquor store: a place where people can and maybe are *expected* to show up messy and disheveled. A place where we can be free of judgment because everyone there is acutely aware of his or her need for Jesus; where those who pass through the door

> We do not like to be uncomfortable. We want a nice, tame Jesus. We want to keep grace in our pocket.

are free to be needy, desperate mess-ups, looking for hope in Jesus rather than the next buzz. A place where we can be honest about how many times we have failed throughout the week.

I love God's people, but the community within the church all too often becomes about us and what we look like, not about who Christ is and what he has done for us. We lay out a specific standard of what a nice Christian should act like, dress like, or speak like, and then we expect everyone to live up to our expectations. This way of community (which isn't really community at all) leaves no room for screwups and shortcomings to be exposed, sin to be confessed, or hearts to be mended. Such environments suffocate believers and often deny them the healing they long for.

> **Grace** is not just a nice word that helps us get through our day; it's the only reason we exist. It's the very air we breathe.

Just imagine what the community of the church would be like if we all laid bare our messes before one another. It's a scary thought, isn't it? It would be hard work; it would force us to be long-suffering with one another. It would force us to free-fall into grace. Yet it would be a beautiful picture of what the church really is: sinners in need of a great Savior. Messy? Yes. But imagine the healing culture that the church could have if we all understood that we are just as pathetic as the person sitting next to us in the pew.

> Yes, the church is a mess, but we are **his** Beloved Mess, and his work will continue to be done through us, despite our mess.

The reality is that the church is only comprised of weak and messy Christians—whether they're admitting it or not! "None is righteous, no, not one; no one understands; no one seeks for God. All have turned aside; together they have become worthless; no one does good, not even one" (Rom. 3:10–12). And, yet, these are the very people that God *delights* in using. Yes, the church is a mess, but we are *his* Beloved Mess, and his work will continue to be done through us, despite our mess.

So, although there are many ways the church needs to change, we need not despair. The church has always been a mess, and it always will be. What the church needs is more people who are brave enough to admit their mess and dive headfirst into the ocean of grace and invite others into the joy of a life of forgiveness and unearned love.

Running from Grace

Because I struggle to accept my messiness, my first response when I've blown it is to run and run hard. I run and hide because the shame of my dysfunction is more than I can handle.

I don't know why I struggle so much. I don't know why I can't seem to move past the waves of fear, anxiety, and depression that

I often live in. I don't know why God continues to allow me to struggle this way. It is the thorn in my flesh, my overarching weakness, and the most frustrating, humbling part of my life. It pains me to even admit to you that this is a part of me.

I don't want to admit that I really am *that bad*. The problem is that I often run to myself where I find only harshness, self-hatred, and anger, instead of running to the cross where I find love, acceptance, and unending patience. I rail against myself and try to improve, only to be met with failure, which simply provides me with a shovel to dig deeper into the pit I've already fallen into.

> The very moment that I am sure I have infuriated God is the exact moment that gives him reason to love me all the more.

The thing about God is that his entire gig is about pursuing us with a red-hot relentless love. He loves to grab mess-ups like you and me by the neck and pluck us out of our self-absorbed pursuit to find approval within ourselves and hold on to us until we finally stop kicking.

And do you know what? The fact that God refuses to leave me alone often inflames a hothead like me. It angers me to be loved when I know that I don't deserve it. I want to earn my way, prove that I'm worthy of his gracious outpouring on me. But that wouldn't be grace, would it? I love to be able to say to people, "But you have no idea what I've done." I'm the queen of "yeah, buts" when it comes to being counseled. I can't do that with God; I can't get away with saying that. The moment that I've said it I've just given him reason to love me all the more. Of course he knows what I've done! Of course he still loves me! His grace is stubborn and it refuses to give up on me no matter how hard I try to prove I don't deserve it. The very moment that I am sure I have infuriated God is the exact moment that gives him reason to love me all the more.

The Day Love Pursued

All four of my kids have at one time or another struggled terribly with going to school. I think I cried just about every day the first year that they were all finally there full-time. Every morning was a battle. And just about every afternoon when I picked them up I had all of their teachers walking toward my car wanting to discuss their day with me before I could even turn off the engine. It was emotionally exhausting, and I carried much guilt and shame over my messy family. We were doing our best at home with our children, but all the world could see was their lack of self-control, stubbornness, and emotional breakdowns.

There was one particularly difficult day that I will never forget. My son was in second grade and quite tired of being told what to do. We had been having some discipline problems with him that we were working through, so it was not surprising that he had blown up at his teacher and told her that he hated her that day. As he stood in line after recess he began to bounce the ball that he was holding. His teacher kindly asked him to hold the ball. This one little request was his tipping point. He bounced the ball as hard as his little arms possibly could and took off running. The principal was standing nearby and caught sight of him as he headed off campus, and thus began an on-foot pursuit of my rogue eight-year-old. My son barely made it out the gates of the school before the man tackled him. He was then carried back to the school office, where the principal sat with his arms wrapped tightly around my kicking and screaming son, repeating these words, "I will not let you go. I will not let you go. I will not let you go." The struggle was so fierce that the office staff called me in for backup.

When I heard that my son had tried to run away and was throwing another one of his outrageous fits, I was angry. Thank God that we lived twenty minutes from the school because after the week that I had already had with him, I'm not sure how I would have handled the situation had I not had that time to cool off. My drive there was filled with desperate thoughts. *How could he embarrass me like this? What are we doing wrong? Why can't he just get his act together and do what he is told?*

Something beautiful happened on the twenty-minute drive into town. The Lord began to soften my heart toward my little boy. He began to show me how I often act very much like my son was acting, but I just hide it better. I thought about Jesus's unrestrained love for me in the way that he relentlessly pursues and tackles me every time I try to run. He holds me while I kick and scream and tells me "I will not let you go" over and over and over again.

I arrived at the school to a tear-faced, mussed-hair boy in the arms of an exhausted principal who had been committed to holding my son down until I got there. And by God's grace my heart just wanted to love him. And so I did. I took him to the car and we went to lunch. We didn't even talk about what happened. We just ate our fries and made jokes. We enjoyed each other for the first time all week.

After bringing him back to the school to finish his day, I sat in the parking lot wondering if I had done the right thing. My son had run away from school, and I took him out to lunch. Everything I've ever known and had been told as a parent told me to do the opposite. For once I stopped listening to everything that everyone was shouting at me about how to raise my children and I just listened to God. My son had heard enough of the law of "try harder and do better," and he broke. It was time for him to know that he was loved, even if he never got any better. No strings attached.

Little did I know that God wasn't done teaching me about grace that day. When our family piled in the car to go out for the evening, I noticed that the dog was missing. It was dusk and our little dachshund was off running in the countryside chasing rabbits, oblivious to the fact that she was coyote bait. We couldn't leave without finding her. My four kids and I spotted her in a field down the road and immediately jumped from the car and raced after her. She had caught the scent of a rabbit and was oblivious to the mob that was hunting her down. For close to an hour we chased her and pleaded with her to come back. As the sun began to fade we grew more and more concerned, and our calling and pleading and searching became more intense. We had already lost several animals to coyotes that year and were not about to give up on her.

The pursuit ended with a desperate tackle and our little dog locked tight in the arms of my daughter. We had given up our evening plans because of the search, and thorny stickers had vandalized our socks and shoelaces, but we had our little friend back safe in our arms. The hugs and attention that she received that night were a picture of Jesus's tenderness toward us. Nobody punished the dog. We were just happy that she was home safe.

I remember that day fondly as "The Day Love Pursued." If my little family was willing to give up a piece of themselves for one little dog, or the principal of the school was willing to tackle my son, how much more does Jesus relentlessly pursue those who are running; those who have their nose stuck to the rabbit trail, oblivious to his call?

Romans 5:8 says, "But God shows his love for us in that while we were still sinners, Christ died for us."

Did you read that? *While* you were *sinning* God came after you! While you were still selfishly pursuing your own interests, binging and purging, finding your worth in your work, cutting your own body, using people for sex, indulging in pornography, overeating, abusing alcohol, turning over to drug addiction, and giving God and the rest of the world a cantankerous kiss-off, he was stubbornly seeking to redeem you. The Hound of Heaven hunted you down in the midst of your unrighteousness. And he continues to pursue you. This is how he shows his love for you. He continues to chase after you every time you bolt.

You have been God's all along. There is no escaping his tight grip, no matter how big your mess is. He is holding on tight, whispering in your ear, "I will not let you go. I will not let you go. I will not let you go." This is good news!

FOR THE JOURNEY

1. What are the things in your life that make you want to run from God?
2. How does knowing that God seeks you out in your mess help you when you want to run?
3. In what ways do you hear God saying, "I will not let you go"?

Doubt Is Not a Dirty Word

All the persons of faith that I know are sinners, doubters, uneven performers. We are secure not because we are sure of ourselves but because we trust that God is sure of us.

Eugene Peterson

We should be unafraid to doubt. There is no believing without some doubting, and believing is all the more robust for having experienced its doubts. Kahlil Gibran put it beautifully, "Doubt is a pain too lonely to know that faith is his twin brother." I like that. If doubts are not the opposite of faith, we can be a bit more open and honest about them with ourselves, others, and God.

Justin Holcomb

"Lord, I believe; help my unbelief" is the best any of us can do really, but thank God it is enough.

Frederick Buechner

The older I get, the more I wonder why I am here. What's the point to all of this? Is the gospel story really true? And every morning my prayer is just like that of the desperate father in Mark 9 crying out for Jesus to help his demon-possessed son when nobody else could: "I believe; help my unbelief!"

Chad Bird beautifully expresses my prayer of unbelief in these words from his book *Christ Alone*.

> Lord, I believe. Help Thou my unbelief. That is our table prayer, our bedside prayer, our office prayer, our going-to-the-movies prayer, our 24/7 petition. Lord, I do believe, but I also don't believe. I am a cocktail of contradictions: double-hearted, fork-tongued, pulled heavenward and hellward every step I take. I fear you but I fear failure. I trust you but I also trust myself. I love you but I also love the limelight. Lord, I believe. Help Thou my unbelief.[1]

I recently turned forty and feel as if every day since then has been an existential crisis at some level. For some of you forty may seem old and for some of you it seems really young. To me it is frighteningly smack-dab in the middle. I'm past the youthful optimism that comes before life has had a chance to beat you down and am now looking squarely into the face of reality—the reality that this is my life and many of the dreams from my youth will never be realized. The reality that tells me there are no do-overs, repeats, or second chances in a world that is screaming "YOLO!" (you only live once) in my face. It's not that I am unhappy; I have a great life. It's just that I've hit the . . . well, I don't even know. Maybe I'm just starting to get tired.

It seems to me that the older I get, the more I sin.[2] I thought I'd be getting better by now. After all, I was told that the Christian life is about getting better and better every day in every way, but I'm not. And when I notice that I'm not getting better, I begin to take things into my own hands and push to change myself. Of course the change only lasts for a few days until I'm tired and then I seem to sin more than I did before! I start doubting that God really has the power to change me. I doubt that the gospel really is true and that I don't have to live a life of self-salvation projects. I doubt that he loves me.

I know in my head that God is for me and not against me. I know the theological answers for my doubts. I could give you a long list of verses that prove the security of my salvation, yet my heart often refuses to follow my head. It's as if my head

> I was told that the Christian life is about getting better and better every day in every way, but I'm not.

and my heart are a mile apart. I know the truth, but I don't feel it. Thankfully not one ounce of whatever doubts I may have, whether they be personal or theological, disqualifies me from God's love.

Why You Shouldn't "Fake It until You Make It"

If you have been a Christian for any length of time you have likely experienced doubt in one form or another. Doubt comes in different varieties for different people. There are the more personal doubts that God really isn't as good as he says he is; that maybe his promise to never leave you or forsake you really isn't true. *Does God really love me? Does he really care about what is going on in my life? Am I really saved?* Then there are the theological mistrusts and queries. *Is there really a God? Is Jesus really God and not just a good man? Is the Bible really God's inspired Word?*

The problem with faith is that there are many questions that just won't be answered this side of heaven. Francis Spufford boldly admits,

> I don't know if there's a God. (And neither do you, and neither does Professor Dawkins, and neither does anybody. It isn't the

kind of thing you can know. It isn't a knowable item.) But then, like every human being, I am not in the habit of entertaining only the emotions I can prove. I'd be an unrecognizable oddity if I did.[3]

Maybe you don't express your doubts as boldly or desperately as I have, but you have likely entertained some of these questions. If so, I want to assure you that your reservations cannot separate you from the love of God. Doubt is not a salvation disqualifier. Hope in the direction of Christ is all the belief that you and I need. In fact, it is your doubt that makes you even more aware of your need for a rescuer, which can be viewed as a sign of Christian maturity.

> The problem with faith is that there are many questions that just won't be answered this side of heaven.

Unfortunately, these words are most likely not the words that you will hear from the pulpit or from other Christian leaders. It seems that oftentimes we are made to feel that mature Christians wouldn't dare question God's love or existence, even in the slightest. We have even been abusively told that if we have reservations about the Bible or about God, then perhaps we are not really saved. (Doubters have already beaten their heads against the wall with the same self-accusation.) Many Christians fear that if they say it's okay to ask questions and to doubt, then others are going to plunge into unbelief and walk away. We're often told, "Be strong so that people can see how strong your God is." But this is not Christianity. Christianity in all of its realness makes the claim, "We are weak, but look at how strong our God is."

The word *doubt* is often met with hushing, as if anyone who hears of your questions will contract a bad case of the doubts just by listening to your uncertainties. Doubters are told to try harder to have more faith. They are told to "just believe," "fake it until you make it," or "trust God like Jesus trusted his Father."

My favorite has always been, "Even if none of this is true, even if there is no God after all, living the Christian life is better than the alternative." I have heard this one a million times over; I've heard it so many times that I've adopted it into my own vernacular. It's what I say apologetically when I'm too proud to say, "I don't know." It's basically saying the same thing as "Fake it until you make it." But it has a special twist! It's as if you are saying, "Fake it and *hope* that you will make it." Where is the hope in faking our way through life? Where is the hope in pretending to believe?

It was the "Fake it until you make it" statement that made me give up on Christianity for an entire year in my early thirties. I was a young mother with four kids six and under, and doubts of God's goodness, mercy, and love consumed me. I was overwhelmed, depressed, suffering from chronic pain and illness, and through some difficult trials had been slapped in the face with the reality of what it was like to live in this sin-cursed world. These doubts soon led me to question if there really was a God.

> It seems that oftentimes we are made to feel that mature Christians wouldn't dare question God's love or existence, even in the slightest. We have even been abusively told that if we have reservations about the Bible or about God, then perhaps we are not really saved.

I had been living a terribly legalistic life believing that Christianity was all about rule keeping and crown polishing. There was no room for Jesus in my Bible. Every word I highlighted was a command. Every time I sat down to read my Bible all I saw was the crushing law that I fell so short of. I was trying really hard to be the Proverbs 31 woman that I thought I was supposed to be. I even resorted to reading Proverbs 31 every morning, hoping for some change. Of course I failed the first day when I wasn't able to get out of bed before dawn because I had been up with the baby (unless you count that 3:00 a.m. feeding). I tried so very hard. But I just couldn't keep it up. I was tired of pretending. I was tired of running around, broom in hand, sweeping all of my failures under the rug so that I would fit in with the shiny, happy Christians—or at least appear to fit in. In my exhaustion, I spiraled into a depression that nearly took my life.

I couldn't fake it anymore because I knew that I *wasn't* making it. The life I was living didn't seem worth it. To me, the alternative to this kind of living certainly *was* a whole lot better, so I quit. I quit Christianity. I quit praying. I quit trying to figure out if God was really there. I quit trying to earn his love. I didn't even care if he loved me. For an entire year I threw my efforts into living as if there was no God.

At the end of that year God showed me that he really does exist, really does care, and really is present in my life, but it took a tragedy to break through to my cynical heart.

My friend Mark had a horrific motorcycle accident. He lay in a coma for a month before we all huddled around his hospital bed, embracing each other as we watched the doctors remove the life support, holding our own breaths as he struggled for his last. I remember so clearly putting his lifeless hand in mine, saying good-bye, then walking out of the room and straight to the prayer chapel of the hospital. I sat down and sobbed as unintelligible words forced their way through my lips. It was the first time I had talked to God that year. It was repulsive, but it was progress.

I continued to talk to God in the days following Mark's death. I told him that I hated him for leaving Mark's twenty-nine-year-old wife to raise their six-year-old son alone. I railed against him for his lack of concern for our hurt and for a life with so much sadness. I was vile. He listened. I was irate. He was patient. I tried to make him run away but he just kept running toward me.

On a sunny February afternoon Mark's family and friends stood mute on a grassy knoll, under an imposing pine tree, permanent markers in hand. Before us lay a simple, unstained wooden box that held Mark's soulless body. Each of us sent him off by writing one final message. As if I were signing a yearbook, mine simply read, "I hope I will see you again." It wasn't eloquent for someone who calls herself a writer, but at the same time it said so much. It was my first glimpse of hope. And as I stepped around the coffin, reading the messages from those who held Mark so close, I began to see something beautiful. There was a confidence in their words. With colored Sharpies they were boldly approaching a throne of grace that I had forsaken. Their words were giving life to my dying soul while we prepared to bury the dead. Through the pain and the sadness I was beginning to see God again.

> Spiritually speaking, I grew more in that year—when I turned away from God— than I had in my entire Christian walk prior. I learned that Christianity wasn't about the strength of my faith but rather the strength of the one in whom my faith rests.

I looked away as they lowered the casket into the ground. I couldn't stand the finality of the burial. I raised my head and spotted a hawk circling directly above us. And then the truth that I had forsaken over the past year came flooding back—Christ is faithful even beyond the here and now. The ground beneath that pine tree was not Mark's final resting place. Like the hawk, he was soaring above, celebrating at the feast of the Lamb, resting in the arms of the one who loved him most. God had spoken and I had finally listened. He had been faithful even when I was not.

Learning more about God's faithfulness did not answer all of my questions, and it didn't cure my forgetfulness of God's goodness. No, it has simply been a monument of God's faithfulness toward me that I go back to time and time again (see Josh. 4:1–24).

Second Timothy 2:13 says, "If we are faithless, he remains faithful for he cannot deny himself." These words were never truer in my life than during that year. Not only did God hold on to me while I tried to run, but he loved me and changed me. He taught me that all of my doubts and unbelief did not make me hopeless, they made me human. Spiritually speaking, I grew more in that year—when I turned away from God—than I had in my entire Christian walk prior. I learned that Christianity wasn't about the strength of my faith but rather the strength of the one in whom my faith rests.

Christ's Strong Faith

The weakest believer among us receives the same strong Christ as does the believer whose faith seems unmoved. This is good news for all of us because it's not the strength of our faith that gives us hope; it's the strength of Jesus's faith. Let me explain.

One summer my family was invited to enjoy a day of waterskiing and lounging on the lake with some friends. The lake was choppy and with each passing speedboat came a wake that caused a big thump and jolt of our boat, which subsequently elicited a scream from my then four-year-old son. He clung desperately to the floor of the boat while I lounged across the padded seats working on my tan and trying to hide my amusement.

You see, he had very little faith in our safety as we hit those large bumps in the water. However, having grown up waterskiing and spending my days on ski boats, I knew that we were perfectly safe. I had complete faith that those wakes that were tossing us from side to side were merely bumps and that the boat was certainly strong enough to endure them. My calm demeanor—feet propped up and drink in hand—showed my trust. I could relax. My child, however, showed very little faith as he screamed with each wave and ripple.

We couldn't have been more different: me, a grown woman with full assurance, knowing that we were safe, showing my confidence in the boat, free to enjoy the sun and spray splashing up on me; and him, my four-year-old, huddled on the floor trying to eat a granola bar, certain that it was his last meal. My faith in the boat was unshakable while my son's was just barely hanging by a thread. And yet here we were, two souls on the same strong boat, heading toward the same destination.

Here's the big question: Did the strength of our faith make any difference in the strength of the boat? Of course not. The boat's strength was not affected by how much faith either of us had put in it on that particular day. It wasn't weakened by my son's doubt, nor was it strengthened by my confidence.

Just as the boat was immovable and never swaying in its ability to bring us safely home, Christ remains our strength even when doubts fill our minds and our faith wavers. In fact, it's Christ's faith we stand on! It's his strength that gets us through and not our own. Christ's life was one constant stream of unwavering faith. Even though he had the power to abandon the mission at any moment, he continued on in humility and perfect faith to fulfill God's redeeming plan. Knowing the pain that was to come, he pleaded with his Father to let the cup pass from his lips (Luke 22:42). As the answer became clear—that the cup would not pass from him, that he was to be beaten, mocked, and stricken with sorrow at the separation of perfect union with his Father—he remained faithful on our behalf. This has become our record. This is now our strength.

Even in our moments of greatest weakness and doubt, Christ remains our strength, holding us up out of the water, confidently taking each blow from the waves with which life is unrelentingly battering us. When everything around you is falling apart, the job is lost, the child rebels, the spouse falls in love with someone else, the friends who said they'd never leave walk away, life has fallen apart at the seams, and you just don't know how to find hope. All the while Christ is unmoved and you are perfectly safe. He will hold on to you to the very end.

My friends, your strong faith—or, more appropriately, your lack thereof—is not connected to some cosmic feeding tube of God's grace. He does not dole out his love and faithfulness based on the strength of our trust. The gospel assures you that he loves you and is holding on to you whether you are lounging about enjoying a time of confident faith or clinging to the bottom of the boat, waiting for the ride to be over. His perfect faith is counted as yours.

Unfortunately many of us have lived our lives believing that God is a cosmic vending machine while being told that if our faith is strong, we will get good things. We've been lied to and told that it is up to us to be strong and to hold on tight to Jesus—all the while forgetting that Jesus came for the weak. Forgetting that Jesus is holding on to us.

Good News for Doubters

What doubters need to hear is not the law, but the gospel. One simply cannot say to a doubter that he or she must work harder at obtaining more faith. Faith is a gift from God. It is not something that we can conjure up on our own. Do I pray for more faith? You bet I do! Like I said before, "Lord, I believe, help my unbelief" is my daily (as in all-day) prayer!

The law without the gospel brings death to the doubter. It causes us to believe that we are alone in our doubt. It causes guilt and shame over not trusting God enough. After all, if we fully put our trust in him we wouldn't question anything, right? Wrong! Who has ever grown in knowledge and trust by not asking questions?

The gospel—the news that Christ is seeking me in my unbelief—brings life. The good news is that the very reason he came to rescue me is because I just could not ever have enough faith. When we know this it quiets our frightened consciences by reassuring us that whether we doubt our Father or not, he is *never* doubting us. This is the gospel! God is love and he *loves us* dearly!

> The gospel—the news that Christ is seeking me in my unbelief—brings life. . . . Whether we doubt our Father or not, he is **never** doubting us.

As we have seen in previous chapters, once the law has done its terrifying work of bringing us to the end of ourselves, the gospel comes in to resuscitate and to mend the brokenness caused by throwing ourselves up against the wall of unachievable standards. The gospel brings us life and freedom for our questions and fears—all of them. God will not leave us or forsake us as we wrestle with our doubts and fears (Deut. 31:8). His level of commitment to us parallels his level of commitment to the Father. He is all in, even when we aren't or can't be.

The good news of the gospel gives us the courage to be honest about our doubts and our fears without being destroyed by them. When we struggle with unbelief we don't have to sink into a pit. We can rest and wait upon the Lord, knowing that doubt is part of our growth and that he has not forgotten or pushed us away.

Knowing that we are fully justified and safe in our salvation, we can and will cry out the prayer of "I believe; help my unbelief" and will be met only with the love and comfort of the Father.

> The good news of the gospel gives us the courage to be honest about our doubts and our fears without being destroyed by them.

So what do we do when the law says to us, "You don't trust God enough, love him enough or believe him enough"? We look straight at it and say, "You are right. I don't trust enough, love enough, believe enough. That is the very reason why I need Christ's perfect faith on my behalf. Thank you for the reminder."

Or better put by my favorite theologian, Martin Luther,

> When the devil throws our sins up to us and declares that we deserve death and hell, we ought to speak thus: "I admit that I deserve death and hell. What of it? . . . For I know One who suffered and made satisfaction in my behalf. His name is Jesus Christ, the Son of God. Where He is, there I shall be also!"[4]

The battle against the accusations of the law can be wearisome. There are times that I feel strong and feisty and can answer back the way that Martin Luther suggests, and then there are times when I feel that I have lost all hope whatsoever. Weak faith or strong, the Lord will be waiting with open arms when I am called home.

My Friend Bill

I first met Bill when he and I were in a small group at church together. He was an aging man who came faithfully with his younger friend. His prayer requests were always the same: he needed us to pray that God would be patient with him for all of his failings. Bill would never quite open up to us about what those failings were, but I imagine that they were much like mine are, and much like yours as well.

Bill doubted God's love for him, but nobody else in the group doubted that God loved Bill. We knew that God loved him in his mess just the way he was loving us in ours. Shame had wedged itself into Bill's relationship with God, and he often wondered if he was really saved. I have no doubt that he was, and I look forward to sitting down for a nice chat with him when we are reunited.

We often hear beautiful stories of people fully trusting that Jesus is waiting to take their hand on the other side of life—people who are confident that to be with Jesus is better than life itself. But what I heard of Bill's last days was that they were filled with fear and doubt. All the way to the end Bill struggled to make sense of his salvation. He doubted God's love for him. He questioned whether he had loved God enough. But do you know what? Not one of Bill's doubts changed God's mind about him. Bill wasn't ushered into heaven and told to sit in the corner and to be happy that God let him in. No, he was embraced by an ever-loving, ever-expectant Jesus who rejoiced that his son had made it home.

The day Bill died, I remembered reading this excerpt from Barbara Duguid's book *Extravagant Grace*. She says,

> I counsel many people who struggle with assurance and suffer with a faith that is weak. I just can't wait to see the joy in their faces when they finally get to heaven! Those who are blessed with strong faith in this lifetime will wake up to find themselves in glory just as they expected. They knew that it was all true, they trusted in God, and perhaps they rarely experienced a moment's doubt. For others,

however, that moment of their awakening will be worth a fortune to watch. Can you imagine the surprise and delight on their faces to find themselves in heaven after all? On earth they could barely hope that the promises of eternal life were true and that God had actually saved them, and they never felt the joy of it during their lifetime. But once they get to heaven it will all change, and I imagine that they will perhaps spend the first millennium or two in heaven surprised and delighted simply to be there. I can only imagine their joy when they hear the words, "Well done, good and faithful servant. . . . Enter into the joy of your master" (Matt. 25:21). Their joy in heaven will be matched only by the Father's joy in proving once again that the gospel of his Son really is enough to save the weakest and most broken of people.[5]

> Heaven is for the weak and needy—the doubters. Christ is our only ticket in, and it is Christ's strong faith that will get us there, not ours.

Be encouraged, my friends, that there are no second-class citizens in heaven. There is no upper echelon of the spiritually and faithfully elite. Heaven is for the weak and needy—the doubters. Christ is our only ticket in, and it is Christ's strong faith that will get us there, not ours.

The gospel frees us to believe that even on our weakest days, Christ is holding on to us.

FOR THE JOURNEY

1. In what ways have you struggled or are you struggling now with doubt?

2. Have you ever felt the freedom to share your doubts with others? If so, what advice were you given? If not, what fears have held you back from sharing?

3. In what way does the law feed our doubts, and how does the gospel speak to our doubts?

4. How would you counsel someone who is struggling with doubt?

Living in Our Belovedness

I'll call nobodies and make them somebodies; I'll call the unloved and make them beloved. In the place where they yelled out, "You're nobody!" they're calling you "God's living children."

Romans 9:25–26, Message

Define yourself radically as one beloved by God. God's love for you and his choice of you constitute your worth. Accept that, and let it become the most important thing in your life.

Brennan Manning

My only desire is to make these words reverberate in every corner of your being—"You are the Beloved."

Henri Nouwen

If you are anything like me you have spent most of your life looking for someone or something to convince you of your belovedness. I have sought it through "performancism"—believing that my worth was in my performance and that if I did everything well enough I would surely make God, as well as those around me, very happy. Yet somehow deep down inside I knew that my performance was not enough and could never be enough. I have lived (and often still do) in disbelief, or perhaps denial, of my true state of belovedness. I know I am his; I just don't always believe it. Just the other day I found myself telling my pastor that I shouldn't be struggling the way that I do, that I know that theologically God's love for me is not contingent upon my performance, yet I live as though it is. "I should know better!" is often my cry. And in my darkest hours God's love seems to be for everyone else but me.

I can well relate to Henri Nouwen when he speaks of his longing to be convinced of his belovedness.

Though the experience of being the Beloved has never been completely absent from my life, I never claimed it as my core truth. I kept running around in large or small circles, always looking for someone or something able to convince me of my Belovedness. It was as if I kept refusing to hear the voice that speaks from the very depth of my being and says: "You are my Beloved, on you my favor rests." That voice has always been there, but it seems that I was always much more eager to listen to other, louder voices saying: "Prove that you are worth something; do something relevant, spectacular, or powerful, and then you will earn the love you so desire." Meanwhile, the soft, gentle voice that speaks to the solitude of my heart remained unheard or, at least, unconvincing.

That soft, gentle voice that calls me the Beloved has come to me in countless ways. . . . But, somehow, all of these signs of love were not sufficient to convince me that I was Beloved. Beneath all my seemingly strong self-confidence there remained the question: "If all those who shower me with so much attention could see me and know me in my innermost self, would they still love me?" That agonizing question, rooted in my inner shadow, kept persecuting me and made me run away from the very place where the quiet voice calling me the Beloved could be heard.[1]

Nouwen's words give me comfort, because despite having been loved from birth, like him I struggle to believe that I am loved and that I am the Beloved. I have never been abused or neglected, yet I allow the lies in my head that tell me I am not worthy of God's love, that I'm not good enough to experience such a gift, to drown out the truth of my belovedness.

I have come to realize that one of our greatest struggles as Christians is to believe that we truly are loved just as we are. What we are seeking after most—to be loved completely and unconditionally—we already have! The sinful, messy, dirty self we want to hide from the world is loved immeasurably. But it takes some convincing to remind ourselves of this.

> What we are seeking after most—to be loved completely and unconditionally—we already have!

The law, whether it be God's law (big "L" law) or experiential law (little "l" law), is beating on us all day every day. The law tells us: *we are loved if* . . . we have a quiet time, don't lose our temper, serve at the soup kitchen, drive the speed limit, use our time wisely, make our boss happy, have obedient children, and so on. Because we fail[2] at many of those things on a daily basis, we conclude that we are not lovable. This is why we need to hear the gospel: we are loved just as we are, messiness and all. This good news has to be pressed in, ground down deep into our hearts before we even begin to take hold of it. We must preach it to ourselves, have it preached to us, and preach it to others because we will always fall back into believing that God's love for us is based on what we do instead of who he is.

Grace loves us enough to not allow us to believe that it is what we do that earns us God's favor. His grace is a red-hot, unyielding grace that declares that *God's not mad at us*!

The Beloved Doubter

I have a good friend who is a well-known author and speaker. Her platform is that of God's love. It's her desire to share his love with others. Years before we ever became friends, I reluctantly attended one of her conferences entitled "Because He Loves Me." I sat in the back row, arms crossed, and scowled at what I was hearing. She kept telling us that God loved us. She wouldn't stop. She went on and on about the ways that he showed grace to us. And all I could think was, *Yeah right. He loves you. He loves the person next to me. But this isn't for me. How dare you tell me that God loves me when you have no idea who I really am!*

My idea of Christianity was so performance-driven that I believed God only loved those who were good and pure and righteous 100 percent of the time, or maybe even just 85 percent of the time. And although I looked like a stellar Christian from the outside, I knew the real me, the one who was rotting away on the inside. I was sure that I was completely unlovable, especially by God. All a lie, straight from the pit of hell, of course!

I see the same disbelief in my own children at times, especially my youngest son. I work hard to express my love to my kids and most of all to express to them that their parents and God love them in spite of their performance. After all, "if the Gospel is about anything, it is about a God who meets us where we are, and not where we ought to be."[3] And I truly believe this and long for my children to believe it as well.

But something doesn't seem to be getting through to my youngest. Either that or he just really likes to see me suffer. Often when I tell him that I love him he replies, "No you don't." He says this so that I will keep trying to convince him. He wants to hear the words of his belovedness. He wants to be convinced that it is true. And so I tell him over and over and over and over. When he refuses to believe me and I have run out of patience, I finally say, "When you say that I don't love you, you are calling me a liar. I wouldn't tell you that I loved you if I didn't love you. I wouldn't give you good things the way I do if I didn't love you. Be quiet now and just believe that you are loved."

I often say the same thing to God that my son says to me. I demand that he convince me, demand that he prove that I am worthy of his love. I often have to tell myself, "Shut up and just believe that you are loved!" As Robert Capon said, "Believe simply that Somebody Else, by his death and resurrection, has made it all right and you just say thank you and shut up."[4]

Thankfully, God is not like me in the patience department. He is not exasperated by my unbelief. In fact, his patience in showering his love over me never runs dry. He continues to pursue me in my stubbornness. He continues to love me even when I don't believe it, even when I accuse him of lying. And in my greatest times of doubt I must look to the Word that tells me that God cannot lie. That God *is* love.

Remembering these characteristics of God and that Christ died for me when it was my sin that hung him on the cross, when it was me who yelled "Crucify him!" along with the angry mob, when it was me who walked by and spit on him, when it was me who rejoiced to see him suffer and die, causes me to "shut up" and believe that I am truly his Beloved, just like he says I am. If he loved me enough to suffer for me, then surely he has not stopped loving me. He is committed to holding on to me because I am his Beloved.

Chad Bird says,

We are not here because God needed servants. We are not here because God needed glorifying. We are not here because God needed anything. We are here because the God who is love, who is our Father, who created all things in and by his Son, willed us to be his *beloved* children.[5]

Sometimes the truth of our belovedness sticks around for a few hours and sometimes only for a few minutes. I must continually be reminded of the gospel in order to live the life of the Beloved. Author Alan Jones says, "The most difficult part of mature faith is to allow ourselves to be the object of God's delight."[6]

And as Brennan Manning points out, "If in our hearts we really don't believe that God loves us as we are, if we are still tainted by the lie that we can do something to make God love us more, we are rejecting the message of the cross."[7] This is where I am often found, living in functional disbelief of the gospel. I bring all of my "yeah-buts" to God and he simply brushes them aside, puts his finger to my lips, and turns my head toward the cross. "Remember the cross, my love. Remember what I have done for you. I sent my one and only Son to die. That was for you. Even if there were no one else on earth, I would have still made the sacrifice. That's how much I love you. You are a full-fledged recipient of my love. Please believe me and live in the freedom of your belovedness, for this is why my Son had to die."

The Beloved Sufferer

Now perhaps you aren't like my son who is growing up hearing that he is loved. If you have suffered or are suffering at the hands of an abuser, the words that prove your belovedness must be shouted even louder.[8] I hope that Henri Nouwen's words are an encouragement to you. Is it not a relief to hear that although neglect and abuse were not a part of his life or mine, we still struggle to believe that we are loved? In other words, this struggle is the propensity of the whole human race.

I have friends whose lives have been filled with abuse and rejection since very early on. While I cannot begin to relate to their pain, we all struggle with the same core issue; unbelief in our belovedness. We all wake up every morning and have to convince ourselves that we are the Beloved. One friend has even gone as far as having the word *Beloved* tattooed on her wrist so that every morning when she wakes up she has a visible reminder that she is not the hurtful words and attacks that she grew up with, but she is a new creature; she is the Beloved.

Some of us are more sensitive to the depravity of our own hearts, and some have hateful words yelled at us, whether in our heads from the past or cutting through the air in our current home. Whatever your situation, do not lose hope. Whether you believe it or not, you *are* the Beloved. When those around you are walking away in disappointment, when you are falsely accused, when you are lashing back at the hateful words slung at you, Jesus is there, whether you feel his presence or not. He is leaning in. He wants you to hear his sweet voice breaking through the bad, declaring you his Beloved.

> Christ's love for you is not fickle. It's not manipulative or abusive. God is not passive-aggressive or codependent. He has no requirements except that you need him.

Christ's love for you is not fickle. It's not manipulative or abusive. God is not passive-aggressive or codependent. He has no requirements except that you need him. He loves to love you. He is loving and pursuing you at this very moment, whether you want him to or not. It is a constant fight to mute the background noise of the world and of our past or present mess and listen to the Holy Spirit's voice of truth saying, "You are my beloved mess."

There are times when I have attacks of sanity and I am able to believe that I am loved in my mess, and then there are times when my self-righteousness gets in the way and I begin to think that I am better than those around me and that God's love is only for those who are getting it right. It's just another revealing of my heart that hasn't fully grasped the truth that we don't do anything to make God love us. He loves us because he is God.

Known, Loved, Wanted

This truth was brought home to me again recently when I treated my kids to a trip to SeaWorld. As we sat and waited for the dolphin show to start, I did my usual people watching (judging) that I do when in crowds. There was the woman next to me who obnoxiously carried on about the man's umbrella in front of her and how her kids weren't going to be able to see anything. She finally got up and demanded very rudely that he put it away. I thought about how I would have been nicer.

Then there was the man in front of me who was holding up his iPad getting ready to record the show while blocking my view. I was annoyed at first until I remembered my friend doing the same at the school Christmas play. She was recording her kids singing so that she could take it to the hospital to share with her critically ill husband. I'm learning to just watch through people's iPads and assume they are doing the same as my friend.

But it was the woman standing off to the side that held my attention (and my judgment). She seemed to be having a hard time being still, and it was bugging me. She would sit, then stand, then pace. She had the look of a drug addict. The sores on her arms and legs, the jerky movements; by the way she couldn't sit still I assumed she was coming off of her high. It gave my pharisaical heart much pleasure to compare myself to this woman. My thoughts turned to judgments like, *At least I'm not that big of a mess* and *She should get her act together for the sake of her kids.*

If you have learned anything from this book you will agree that according to the law, I really was no better than this woman. It wasn't until she turned around that my heart realized this truth. On her wrist she wore a wide red band with the name *JESUS* printed boldly across it.

Now I don't claim to know this woman's heart, but most people won't don Jesus garb unless they have had some sort of movement toward him. So for that reason I assume that she belongs to him. In God's eyes, this woman who seemed to be a huge outward mess was no different from me.[9] She too was part of the Beloved.

I wondered if perhaps that day was another in a string of hard days for her; a day of detox spent at an amusement park to keep her mind distracted. I don't know. But what I do know is that I needed Jesus just as much as she did that day. And every day. God wasn't finished with her yet, just as he is not yet finished with me.

Remembering this changed my thoughts from judgment to compassion. I suddenly wanted to know this woman's story. And though I'm quite reserved and not much of a hugger, I wanted to jump up and embrace this sister and tell her that she wasn't alone, that she was loved.

> We live in a broken world where drugs destroy, parents abuse, spouses cheat, pastors fail, children rebel, dreams shatter, and death devastates. For some it is a world in which there doesn't seem to be any hope for change. But this is not the end. Grace always has the last word for the Beloved.

We live in a broken world where drugs destroy, parents abuse, spouses cheat, pastors fail, children rebel, dreams shatter, and death devastates. For some it is a world in which there doesn't seem to be any hope for change. But this is not the end. Grace always has the last word for the Beloved.

Jesus is inviting each one of his Beloveds—the doubters, the imposters, the self-righteous like me, and the drug addicts like the woman at SeaWorld—to join him at the feast. He desires us based on his love for us, not on our merit. And that is often a hard truth for us to grasp. We want to pay our way with our goodness, or at least our *I'm-better-than-the-person-next-to-me*-ness.

> Jesus leans in with compassion when the rest of the world walks away in disgust. When everyone seems to pull away in disappointment, Jesus listens to our ugliness, leans forward, and whispers, "You are my Beloved."

Living in our belovedness means that we can take our hands out of our pockets; our money is worthless in God's economy. We are in with him; there are no bribes, no tips, and no annual dues. He has paid our way and the tab is clear. We have full access to the Father and don't need to be slipping Jesus a twenty to get us a good seat. We have a personal invitation. He wants us at his banquet, not just as a guest but as his friend. He meets us at the door and takes us to the seat right beside him. He sits down with us and looks deeply into our eyes as we talk. His gaze makes us feel instantaneously known and loved, and we have no need to look away, for our shame and guilt are gone. All of the discomfort of our vulnerability has dissipated into the confident knowledge that this man is for us in every way imaginable. He leans toward us as we share the ugliness of our hearts. He already knows. Nothing surprises him or shocks him. He has no need to pull away.

We are known.

We are loved.

We are wanted.

He leans in and he loves.

Jesus is the only one who knows us completely yet never wishes that we were something other than who we are. Jesus leans in with compassion when the rest of the world walks away in disgust. When everyone seems to pull away in disappointment, Jesus listens to our ugliness, leans forward, and whispers, "You are my Beloved."

Living Loved

Maybe you have read this chapter and you have been like me, sitting in the back row, arms crossed, shaking your head, with the argument *But you don't know what I have done or who I am* reverberating through your being. Don't lose hope, friend. These words are for you. The words I speak are coming from a sinner. Not a G-rated, "I didn't do a quiet time and I didn't kiss my husband good-bye this morning" kind of sinner, but an R-rated, neighbor-hating, lustful-thinking, cursing-at-the-dog kind of sinner.

I wake up every morning trying to prove that I am worthy of a love that I already have. I sin, I screw up, and I run to compose myself. I often fail to believe that God loves me just as I am. I often believe that I have to spend my day proving my faith, proving that I was worth dying for.

In his book *Adam: God's Beloved*, Henri Nouwen aptly describes the struggle that we all have in claiming our belovedness:

> Each one of us is unique, known by name, and loved by the One who fashioned us. Unfortunately, there is a very loud, consistent, and powerful message coming to us from our world that leads us to believe that we must prove our belovedness by how we look, by what we

have, and by what we can accomplish. We become preoccupied with "making it" in this life, and we are very slow to grasp the liberating truth of our origins and our finality. We need to hear the message announced and see the message embodied, over and over again. Only then do we find the courage to claim it and to live from it.[10]

It is when we remember the gospel—the good news that Christ came and lived the life that we could never live, died the death that we deserve, and endured the agonizing separation from his Father that we will never have to experience—that we can finally begin to believe that we are loved.

The good news is that no matter how badly we've blown it (and we all have) or how unlovable we have been (and we all are), our belovedness is not measured by how well we have done or how lovely we are.

Our lovability is not based on our actions; it is based on God being God and loving us as we are because of the righteousness of his Son. Whether we believe it or not, we are his Beloved. Doesn't that just make you breathe a sigh of relief? The whole world (and often the church) is constantly telling us that we must earn love, that we must prove ourselves lovable. The gospel flips all of that upside down and tells us that we are loved not despite ourselves, but for who we really are, mess and all. God takes the whole package and wraps it in Christ's robe and lavishes upon us every ounce of affection that he has toward his Son.

Living in our belovedness means knowing that we can't mess it up, that we are the Beloved, no matter our performance.

Living in our belovedness means living in the truth that there is nothing that we can do to make him love us any more or any less than he already does.

Living in our belovedness means taking a deep breath, knowing that God, in all his sovereignty, is in control and has us on his mind all the time.

Living in our belovedness means knowing that we are going to be okay even when we don't feel okay.

Living in our belovedness means knowing that Jesus is leaning in while the rest of the world is walking away.

Believe you are loved and live in the freedom of your belovedness.

FOR THE JOURNEY

1. In what ways do you find it difficult to believe that you are God's Beloved?

2. How does the law contribute to our feelings or beliefs that we are unloved when we mess up?

3. Christ "leans in" instead of away from us when we have really messed up. What makes this possible?

Kissed by Grace

And here in dust and dirt, O here
The lilies of His love appear!

Henry Vaughan

God writes the gospel not in the Bible alone, but on trees
and flowers and clouds and stars.

Martin Luther

I know nothing, except what everyone knows—if there when
grace dances, I should dance.

W. H. Auden

Perhaps you've come to this last chapter wondering, *Where's the application, Kimm? I've read your entire book, but I'm still a mess!*

I too love to be told how I can clean up my act. My law-loving heart wants to have some skin in the game. But if I were to end this book by giving you a list of things to do or by telling you to go out and be better, I would be sending you right back to the law, which is death. And really, I'd rather not kill off my readers.

I see this closing chapter as my last chance to share the life-giving message of the gospel. I long to hear the prison doors swing wide as you experience the freedom of knowing that you are his Beloved.

It is often hard for us to see God working in the midst of our messes. We sometimes believe that he is a deadbeat dad, abandoning us or ignoring us in our greatest time of need. But the opposite is true. We often see grace more clearly when we are at our worst. That's certainly been the case for me.

I'd had it. It was the end of a long day at the end of a long week, and I was done. All of the whining and fighting and complaining coming from my four kids had come to a head. I don't remember what the tipping point was, but I guarantee that my response was a complete overreaction to my kids' actions. It was one of those take-cover-because-Mom-is-going-to-blow moments. And I did just that. Every child was sent to their room as ugliness spewed from my lips. Before I knew it, the words were gone, a vapor I could not grasp and stuff back in. My anger sent me storming down the hall with one final announcement: "I can't do this anymore!" It was there that my husband stepped out in front of me. I pushed him to the side, wanting nothing more than to make it out the door and to my car where I could go drive off the anger on some back country roads, but he stepped back in front of me, this time grabbing tight, determined not to let me go. I waited for his words of disappointment, words of correction or defense of the kids, but the only words that came were "I love you" followed by an unrelenting and reassuring embrace.

I realized in that moment of ugliness that I was loved as I was. I didn't have to run and hide in shame. I melted into his arms, thankful for the safe place that I had found.

My husband's unexpected and undeserved grace for me in that moment changed everything. Instead of running away, I found myself seeking forgiveness. Instead of withholding affection, I found myself pouring out love. One act of love changed the trajectory of my entire response. I had once again been kissed by grace.

I am not the only one who has stories about the difference grace makes. Grace changes everything. *Everything!* From the way that you relate to and care for those around you, forgiving and loving without expectations, to the grace that you give yourself, not beating yourself up with self-condemnation when you have failed.

> Grace changes everything. **Everything!** From the way that you relate to and care for those around you, forgiving and loving without expectations, to the grace that you give yourself, not beating yourself up with self-condemnation when you have failed.

If you sat and talked with my friends Rob and Erika (from chapter 4), you would hear story after story of how they were loved and accepted in the midst of their mess. This isn't always the way life plays out. We don't often receive grace from others when we have really screwed up, but if you look carefully you will begin to see the stories of radical grace all around you. These are the kisses on the cheek, graces on the ground, that point us to the only one who shows grace, love, and acceptance every time our mess is exposed. He knows no other way.

Here are a few more stories from the lives of others who have been kissed by grace:

Grace for the LEGO Thief

"See what great love the Father has lavished on us, that we should be called children of God." (1 John 3:1)

I saw a beautiful example of the lavishness of love and forgiveness one day through my six-year-old son. He had received a letter in the mail from his little friend who had recently been at our house for a Christmas party. Upon opening the letter, four LEGO pieces spilled out into his lap. He was ecstatic, because in his world one can never have too many LEGOs, and he thought this was a great gift from his five-year-old friend, Jacob. Included in the envelope was a note. In the efforts of good parenting, Jacob's mom had written an apology and had her son trace the letters. It read: "Do you forgive me for stealing your LEGOs?"

Apparently this little guy was in the habit of pocketing LEGOs and small toys while playing in other kids' bedrooms, and his mom has had to do this before.

My son immediately ran to get a piece of paper and scribbled a giant "YES" across the top. He then proceeded to write "I LOVE YOU" as big as he possibly could to "make sure that his friend knew he wasn't mad." The words on the page were then decorated with pictures of Joshua and Jacob holding hands and playing LEGOs together.

And as if the cuteness and the profundity of the letter were not enough, my son disappeared into his room and returned with a handful of LEGOs. He then took the four stolen LEGOs, added six more, and built a robot for his friend. He was returning a request for forgiveness with far more than little Jacob had ever anticipated. Not only did my son forgive Jacob, but he also lavishly loved him by giving back what he had stolen, and more!

This is grace! Although God deals with us on a much greater level, this is a sweet reminder of what it is to be forgiven. It is so much more than a "yes" to our plea for forgiveness; it is a flood of kindness and generosity made available to us through his Son.

Grace for the Junkie

Jeff lived on the streets and spent his days getting high, always looking for his next hit, terrified of what might happen if he ever came down. I run a halfway house ministry where we help addicts like Jeff get into rehabilitation centers to get clean and sober and back on their feet. I'd been trying to help him for a long time, but he didn't seem to see a need for rescue. His love of the "high life" kept him on the streets and got him into serious trouble. I was often frustrated with him and his lack of desire to change and found myself wanting to write him off, thinking that my time might be more useful to someone who wanted to work on getting their act together.

One day Jeff came in to see me. He stumbled in high and stinking of cheap liquor. His eye was swollen shut and blood trickled down from a wound on his eyebrow. His nose was broken and he had a front tooth missing. Apparently things had not gone well for him when he tried to buy his dope that day. He was attacked and beaten, left lying on the sidewalk as the dealer stepped over him, taking off with his money and his next hit.

I just looked at him in disgust. I wanted to tell him that it served him right, that if he would listen to me and let me help him these kinds of things wouldn't happen anymore. But I was interrupted by Andy, the bar owner from next door, who had looked out his window and seen Jeff's bloody face as he walked by. He was coming to see if Jeff was okay.

Andy sat down next to Jeff, put his arm around him, and asked him to tell him the whole story. Jeff just sat and cried in defeat. He was so sick of himself that he wanted to die.

And instead of telling Jeff all of the ways that he needed to change, the way that I would have, Andy just sat and listened. Then, much like the father who ran to embrace his prodigal son, totally disregarding the filth of his clothes, the stench of his person, and the hurt he had caused, Andy offered Jeff a shower, some fresh clothes, and a warm meal.

Andy showed me what grace really looks like. It looks like love. Jeff is six months clean to this day, thanks to the love of a bar owner.

The greatest discovery that I have made while working with getting addicts into rehab has been that the law never works to rescue them. You can tell them what to do until you are blue in the face, but it cannot give them the power to overcome their enslavement to their addiction. Every time an addict is told to try hard to quit, it pushes them to only look within themselves to find the strength to do something that man is incapable of: salvation.

Only God can free them from the chains of enslavement. They must admit that they are powerless and unable to save themselves. It is then that the gospel can come in and begin its restorative work. I've seen it over and over again. It's all grace.

Grace for the Reluctant Relative

My grandfather recently died. I was devastated.

I didn't want to go to the memorial. I hate the vulnerability that comes with saying good-bye. The open crying and hugging are enough to make me want to run the other direction; and that's just what one family member tried to do. It was just too much sadness for her. She didn't think that she was strong enough to do the hard business of coming and grieving and missing Grandpa, so she said "no." I was jealous. I wish that I could have done the *same. The entire family texted and called, urging her to come and be with us, but she just wouldn't budge.*

The dreaded hour of the memorial service came, and we all gathered in the church to say our good-byes to Grandpa, with boxes of tissue in hand. The church was full as expected since my grandpa had an amazing ministry throughout his life, and people had traveled from far away to pay their respects. As we took our seats, I heard a commotion. Suddenly, the entire family began to stand and rush to the side of the church. It was then that I realized that the family member who had been missing had changed her mind and had driven all morning to get there, arriving just in time for the service. Suddenly, the entire family, who had been angry at what they viewed as her selfishness, was rushing to hug her. All of the frustration with this woman dissipated at the sight of her walking through that church door. We were never so happy to see someone who had caused so much pain. Everything that she had said, done, or threatened not to do was thrown to the side and grace rushed in.

There was a huge display of grace in our family that day. A day that showed us a little more about what the love of Christ really is, about what it really means to love and to be loved.

Grace for the Teen without Hope

Things had been exceedingly dark for seventeen-year-old Austin for quite some time. He had tried to voice his desperation to his parents but never felt that he could really be honest about his depression. They were always trying to get him to "cheer up" and "look on the bright side." He was ashamed every time he passed the sign of the church on the corner that read "We Are Too Blessed To Be Depressed." It seemed to be the same message that his parents were preaching at him. Austin knew that he was blessed, but he couldn't figure out why he was so depressed.

135

He had been meeting with the pastor at his church for several months, but it just seemed that all the pastor did was spit out Bible verses that made Austin feel like even more of a failure. Nobody seemed to understand his pain. Not even his girlfriend, Kayla, who soon broke up with him because "his negativity was bringing her down."

Austin was devastated over their breakup. In his mind, Kayla was all he had left to live for, the only thing that made him feel alive. Nothing in life seemed to be worth pursuing now. He hardly left his room.

One day, after a long arduous night in which he sat curled up in a ball in the corner of his room, crying uncontrollably for hours, Austin gave up. He fashioned a noose out of his little sister's jump rope and secured it from the eave right outside his second-story bedroom window. He stepped up onto the window seat, took a deep breath, and slipped the rope around his throat, sliding the knot to the base of his neck. All that was left to do was to step off of the sill. He would finally enter the darkness that had terrified him for so long. No more sleepless nights. No more cruel girlfriends. No more disappointed parents. Just dark.

But as Austin's right foot stepped off to lead the way to his tragic death, his bedroom door swung open. His mom rushed in in horror and carefully grabbed him, slipping the rope from his neck. They both collapsed on the floor and wept.

After a few minutes Austin's mom pulled herself up to her feet. Through tear-wrecked mascara she looked at her son and spoke softly to him. She said, "Let's go out for some lunch." Austin reluctantly pulled on a T-shirt, fearing the lecture that would come from across the table. But he was wrong. As he picked at what used to be his favorite meal, pizza with olives and pineapple, his mom did nothing but tell him how much he was loved. She wouldn't stop. And as she continued to pour words of grace over him, the pizza began to take on flavor. He couldn't remember the last time *that he felt enjoyment over something. He was beginning to get a glimpse of life again as the numbness ever so slowly began to dissolve.*

This one act of grace was the beginning of healing for Austin and his parents. They were able to find a good counselor and the right meds to help him gain back his life. He is now married and expecting his first child.

When I asked Austin what the game changer was for him, he told me, with tear-filled eyes and a cracked voice, "I tried to kill her son, and she took me out to lunch."

Grace Changes Everything

Grace is everywhere. We often find it among the most tragic, most vile, most hopeless situations. But we also find it in the little, mundane, everyday things as well. Though the outcome may not always be what we had hoped for, grace is somehow woven throughout our lives to remind us that we are loved in the midst of the mess. Although we are fragmentary creatures living between the already and the not yet, we are perfectly loved as we are. After all, "spirituality isn't about being finished and perfect; spirituality is about trusting God in our unfinishedness."[1]

> Each story in our lives plays an important role. There are times that we feel kissed by grace and times that we feel abandoned. But although our emotions may tell us otherwise, God has never left us. He loves to love us.

Each story in our lives plays an important role. There are times that we feel kissed by grace and times that we feel abandoned. But although our emotions may tell us otherwise, God has never left us. He loves to love us. In fact, Zephaniah 3:17 tells us that he is with us and rejoicing over us right at this very moment!

> The LORD your God is in your midst,
>   a mighty one who will save;
> he will rejoice over you with gladness;
>   he will quiet you by his love;
> he will exult over you with loud singing.

You are not lost, bedraggled saint. You are not forgotten. Grace is chasing you down to pour out God's love on you. All this time, even in the midst of what may feel like your destruction, God has not let go of you. If you are in Christ, you are cherished, treasured, and, most importantly, his Beloved. While others may have given up on you, or you may have given up on yourself, while your world may be falling apart, you remain in his grip. If you are barely hanging on, don't fret—he is holding on tight to you.

Whether we like it or not, God is going to use every mess that we are in, every mess that we have made or others have made, in order to bring his redemption plan to completion. There are times that these words are a comfort to me and other times that they cause me to weep. But I am not alone in my earthly sorrow. Christ, who is walking through the mess right along with me, has also wept through the pains of this world. This quote, attributed to Robert Capon, encourages us to weep without shame.

> If we must weep our way to heaven, then let us weep and be on our way, for he who is the Way wept too, and despiseth us not.[2]

Your mess is not the end of you. Though the hurt and the pain that you have caused or that others may have inflicted upon you may seem unforgivable, if you are in Christ, you are safe. He is your safe place. He is calling you to himself, not with crossed arms and a tapping foot but with arms uncrossed, stretched out wide, waiting to hold you. Outstretched arms that hung on the cross. The cross where your sin was nailed right next to mine. The cross that took your shame and your guilt and made it all his.

Grace is for the gutter dwellers. Grace is for the vilest of sinners. Grace is for all of us who have forsaken Christ for the momentary pleasure of sin. It's for the sinners and the sinned against. It's for the screwups, the riffraff, the misfits, and the ragamuffins. For those who just don't think they can make it another day. Grace is for the dirty who need to be made clean. That's all of us. And we've all been kissed by grace.

> Grace is for the gutter dwellers. Grace is for the vilest of sinners. Grace is for all of us who have forsaken Christ for the momentary pleasure of sin.

The hope found in this book is not the hope of a better, less messy you, but a hope that sustains you. A hope in the one who lived, bled, and died in order that you may be called his Beloved. A hope that renders you okay when things *aren't* okay. A hope that is with you, riding out the waves of your life through the very end, never giving up on you. A hope that promises you so much more than the messes that you are wading through. "A Hope that counts upon, is kindly raised upon, the mess that you actually are."[3] A hope that has loved you out of death and into freedom.

Robert Capon says,

> We were never told that it would not hurt, only that nothing would ever finally go wrong; not that it would not often go hard with us but that there is therefore now no condemnation to them which are in Christ Jesus.

All Jesus did was announce that truth and tell you it would make you free. It was admittedly a dangerous thing to do. You are a menace. But he did it; and therefore, menace or not, here you stand: uncondemned, forever, now. What are you going to do with your freedom?[4]

And so I end this journey with you, praying that you are encouraged. Not encouraged that you will someday be rid of your mess, but encouraged that you are loved in the midst of it, for you are loved as you are, not as you should be.

Each one of us tattered and bruised saints will someday drag ourselves over the finish line and into the presence of Jesus. And do you know what he will do on that day? He will rush to our side, overjoyed at the fact that we are finally home. Nothing we have ever done will be up for discussion. All of our sins in thought, word, and deed have already been spoken into oblivion, where they can never be called back. We will finally be totally and forever free to enjoy being the Beloved.

It's work to believe that we really are forgiven, loved, and never forgotten. But to hear words of grace and forgiveness spoken through the lips of others and to see them in their stories, as well as our own, gives us hope.

There is a hole in my bedroom wall from a vase that I once threw at my husband in a fit of rage. I could have patched it up and repainted it, but I chose not to. Instead, I found the perfect piece of art to hang over it, covering that shameful reminder of my failure; it simply reads "Love You More."

Though your mess may be deep, your faith may be weak, and your sins may be many, God will always and forever *love you more*. You are his Beloved Mess.

FOR THE JOURNEY

1. In what ways has God met you in your mess throughout the reading of this book?
2. Do you have your own story of how you were kissed by grace in the midst of your mess?
3. Has your view of being messy changed with reading this book? How?
4. What is one takeaway from this book (maybe a phrase or story) that will help you to remember that you are loved as you are?

Appendix

Gospel Truths
for the Beloved

When I am in the middle of the mess, I often find it difficult to weed out the lies that tell me that my worth is in what I do and not in what Christ has done for me and continues to do for me. I lose my way, and my emotions lead me down dark paths that terrify my conscience and trick me into a life lived in functional disbelief of my belovedness. I need to be reminded that he really is there, he really does care, and that I really am his Beloved Mess.

It takes work to remember the truth of God's love for me when I've really blown it, when I am feeling generally weak and faithless, when I am overwhelmed or discouraged, or when I have hurt or have been hurt by others.

I hope you find this appendix a helpful tool as you seek to rest in Christ in the midst of your mess. Rip out these truths and tape them to your bathroom mirror, keep them on your dashboard, tattoo them on your eyelids! Do whatever you need to do in order to be reminded of Christ's love for you.

Gospel Truths for When You've Blown It

Life is full of messed-up, jacked-up, screwed-up moments of failure. No matter how hard we try to be good, there will always be times when we just plain blow it. Times that we show the world just how much we really do need Jesus. What do you do when you blow it? Here are a few gospel truths that help me to get back to the right way of thinking when all I want to do is wallow in my sin.

> **His kindness leads me to repentance:** "Or do you presume on the riches of his kindness and forbearance and patience, not knowing that God's kindness is meant to lead you to repentance?" (Rom. 2:4)
>
> **He is not angry with me:** "Since, therefore, we have now been justified by his blood, much more shall we be saved by him from the wrath of God." (Rom. 5:9)
>
> **He saved me when I was his enemy:** "For if while we were enemies we were reconciled to God by the death of his Son, much more, now that we are reconciled, shall we be saved by his life." (Rom. 5:10)
>
> **Where sin abounds, grace abounds all the more:** "Now the law came in to increase the trespass, but where sin increased, grace abounded all the more." (Rom. 5:20)
>
> **Sin is no longer my master:** "For sin will have no dominion over you, since you are not under law but under grace." (Rom. 6:14)
>
> **Nothing I do can separate me from his love:** "For I am sure that neither death nor life, nor angels nor rulers, nor things present nor things to come, nor powers, nor height nor depth, nor

anything else in all creation, will be able to separate us from the love of God in Christ Jesus our Lord." (Rom. 8:38–39)

My sin has already been forgiven and nailed to the cross: "And you, who were dead in your trespasses and the uncircumcision of your flesh, God made alive together with him, having forgiven us all our trespasses, by canceling the record of debt that stood against us with its legal demands. This he set aside, nailing it to the cross." (Col. 2:13–14)

God is greater than my heart: "By this we shall know that we are of the truth and reassure our heart before him; for whenever our heart condemns us, God is greater than our heart, and he knows everything." (1 John 3:19–20)

There is no more judgment against me: "There is therefore now no condemnation for those who are in Christ Jesus." (Rom. 8:1)

Gospel Truths for When You Are Feeling Weak

The life of the believer is one of constantly seeing our own weakness and running to Christ for his strength. Here are a few gospel truths for when you are feeling weak.

It's okay to be weak: "For the sake of Christ, then, I am content with weaknesses, insults, hardships, persecutions, and calamities. For when I am weak, then I am strong." (2 Cor. 12:10)

His grace is always sufficient and will always be poured out on you in your weakness: "But he said to me, 'My grace is sufficient for you, for my power is made perfect in weakness.' Therefore I will boast all the more gladly of my weaknesses, so that the power of Christ may rest upon me." (2 Cor. 12:9)

The Holy Spirit helps us in our weakness: "Likewise the Spirit helps us in our weakness. For we do not know what to pray for as we ought, but the Spirit himself intercedes for us with groanings too deep for words." (Rom. 8:26)

He understands our weakness: "For we do not have a high priest who is unable to sympathize with our weaknesses, but one who in every respect has been tempted as we are, yet without sin." (Heb. 4:15)

He first loved us in our weakness, so we don't have to prove we are strong to earn his love: "For while we were still weak, at the right time Christ died for the ungodly. For one will scarcely die for a righteous person—though perhaps for a good person one would dare even to die." (Rom. 5:6–7)

It is not until we see our weakness that we will praise his strength:
"I was pushed hard, so that I was falling,
but the LORD helped me.
The LORD is my strength and my song;
he has become my salvation.
Glad songs of salvation are in the tents of the
righteous:
'The right hand of the LORD does valiantly.'"
(Ps. 118:13–15)

Our strength fails but his strength goes on forever:
"My flesh and my heart may fail,
but God is the strength of my heart and my portion forever." (Ps. 73:26)

Gospel Truths for When You Are Discouraged

Being human can be discouraging at times. What can we do when we feel as if we can't go on another minute? Trying harder isn't the answer. Remembering the love and grace that the Father continually pours out on us is the answer. Here are a few verses to encourage your heart during those difficult times.

Wait on the Lord and he will strengthen your heart:

"I would have lost heart, unless I had believed
That I would see the goodness of the LORD
In the land of the living.
Wait on the LORD;
Be of good courage,
And He shall strengthen your heart;
Wait, I say, on the LORD!" (Ps. 27:13–14 NKJV)

Wait for the Lord expectantly:

"From the depths of despair, O LORD,
    I call for your help.
Hear my cry, O Lord.
    Pay attention to my prayer.
LORD, if you kept a record of our sins,
    who, O Lord, could ever survive?
But you offer forgiveness,
    that we might learn to fear you.
I am counting on the LORD;
    yes, I am counting on him.
    I have put my hope in his word.
I long for the Lord
    more than sentries long for the dawn,
    yes, more than sentries long for the dawn.
O Israel, hope in the LORD;
    for with the LORD there is unfailing love.
    His redemption overflows.
He himself will redeem Israel
    from every kind of sin." (Ps. 130 NLT)

He bottles up every tear:

"You have kept count of my tossings;
    put my tears in your bottle.
    Are they not in your book?" (Ps. 56:8)

He loves the brokenhearted:
> "The Lord is near to the brokenhearted
>> and saves the crushed in spirit." (Ps. 34:18)

He will not burden the discouraged heart:
> "A bruised reed he will not break,
>> and a faintly burning wick he will not quench;
>> he will faithfully bring forth justice." (Isa. 42:3)

He is never discouraged even when we are:
> "He will not grow faint or be discouraged
>> till he has established justice in the earth;
>> and the coastlands wait for his law." (Isa. 42:4)

He continues to pour out his mercies on us no matter our circumstances:
> "The steadfast love of the Lord never ceases;
>> his mercies never come to an end;
> they are new every morning;
>> great is your faithfulness." (Lam. 3:22–23)

Even when we are discouraged and our faith is weak, he remains faithful to us: "If we are faithless, he remains faithful—for he cannot deny himself." (2 Tim. 2:13)

Gospel Truths for When Your Heart Hurts

Unless you are a hermit living in a cave in the mountains, you will undoubtedly experience relational difficulties in one way or another. Living as a sinner in a world of sinners, there will be times that you will hurt others or be hurt by others. Here are some verses to help you through those times of pain and confusion.

> **God was for me before I could even speak his name, and he remains for me today:** "What then shall we say to these things? If God is for us, who can be against us? He who did not spare

his own Son but gave him up for us all, how will he not also with him graciously give us all things?" (Rom. 8:31–32)

If God's grace was sufficient to fulfill the law through Christ, then God's grace is sufficient for me today: "For from his fullness we have all received, grace upon grace. For the law was given through Moses; grace and truth came through Jesus Christ." (John 1:16–17)

He will enable you to do what he has called you to walk through: "He who calls you is faithful; he will surely do it." (1 Thess. 5:24)

He holds everything together even when we cannot: "And he is before all things, and in him all things hold together." (Col. 1:17)

He promises to walk with us in trials and will not allow us to be destroyed:

> "When you pass through the waters, I will be with
>   you;
> and through the rivers, they shall not overwhelm
>   you;
> when you walk through fire you shall not be burned,
>   and the flame shall not consume you." (Isa. 43:2)

Acknowledgments

Many people have played instrumental roles in the writing of this book, whether through prayer, texts, emails, sermons, or the hard work of listening to me complain about being a mess. If you have encouraged me in any way throughout this process, please know that I am incredibly grateful for you even if your name is not listed in these acknowledgments.

I would first like to thank my husband, Justin, and my kids, Grace, Jonah, Lily, and Jackson, who have been so patient with me. They have happily eaten more frozen pizzas than any one family should consume, searched patiently for clean underwear when I failed to keep up with the laundry, and endured my distractedness when they desired my attention. Thank you guys for loving me and supporting me throughout the writing of this book.

I would also like to thank my friend and fellow member of The League of the Pathetic, Elyse Fitzpatrick. Elyse has been a human embodiment of God's grace in my life not only throughout the writing of this book but also in all of my messes. She has taught me more than anyone else about using my failures to minister to others. This book would not have happened without her encouragement. Thank you for loving me, E.

And to my other League of the Pathetic friend, Kaye Atkins, for being a roof-ripping friend who continually lowers me to the feet of Jesus when I am too paralyzed by the mess. Thank you, Kaye, for caring for me the way that you do.

To Lauren Larkin, my go-to theologian and this book's biggest cheerleader, who made herself available for theology talk and writing help any time I needed to talk things out. And to Rachel Cohen, Jess Thompson, Jeff Block, and Chad West, who encouraged me greatly and kept me laughing. Thank you.

To my agent, Andrew Wolgemuth, for believing in me and my message and for helping me to get this book into the hands of readers. And to my amazing editor, Liz Heaney, for patiently walking me through the process of making this book what it is and for teaching me how to be a better writer.

To my family at Valley Center Community Church who have cared greatly for our family and faithfully prayed for the writing of this book. And to my extended family of Lamberths and Berrys, every single one of you. Thank you for your unwavering friendship for so many years and through so many messes.

To Curt Benham and Jonathan Adams of Village Church at Vinings, who have ministered to me greatly through their online sermons. You guys rock!

Thank you to *all* of my friends (you know who you are) who have walked and talked and prayed with me throughout the writing of this book. I am blessed to be so well loved.

Notes

Chapter 1 I'm a Mess

1. *Merit monger* is a term used by Martin Luther to refer to the Galatians who had fallen into the belief that they had to earn merit (favor) with God to be justified.

2. For the duration of this book I will refer to myself as a sinner. I am aware that I am considered a saint because I now have the righteousness of Christ. This does not mean that I no longer sin (Romans 7). I hold to what Luther calls *simul justus et peccator*, meaning that at the same time I am just and a sinner. Acknowledging that I am a sinner proves that God's Word is true, that I cannot fulfill the law, and that I need to be rescued.

3. Lori Harding, Twitter post, January 13, 2014, https://twitter.com/loril harding/status/422936896038531073.

4. Simon Tugwell, *The Beatitudes: Soundings in Christian Traditions* (Springfield, IL: Templegate, 1980), 7.

5. Mike Yaconelli, *Messy Spirituality* (Grand Rapids: Zondervan, 2002), 21–22.

6. Henri Nouwen, Donald P. McNeill, and Douglas A. Morrison, *Compassion, A Reflection on the Christian Life* (Garden City, NY: Doubleday, 1983), 21.

Chapter 2 The League of the Guilty

1. I am not at all saying that there isn't a place for reading about parenting or asking older and wiser women for advice; these are not bad things to do. But in the matter of training myself to be a self-righteous mother, they became all that I put my hope in.

2. John T. Pless, *Handling the Word of Truth* (St. Louis: Concordia, 2004), 13.

3. Matthew 22:36–39.

4. Romans 3:10.

5. Romans 3:23.

6. John 3:1–8.
7. Chad L. Bird, *Christ Alone: Meditations and Sermons* (Create Space, 2014), 97.
8. Francis Spufford, *Unapologetic* (New York: HarperCollins, 2013), 46–47.

Chapter 3 The Imposter, Myself, and I

1. Brennan Manning, *Abba's Child* (Colorado Springs: NavPress, 1994, 2002), 56.
2. Woody Allen, epigraph, in Eric Lax, *On Being Funny: Woody Allen and Comedy* (New York: Charterhouse, 1975), ix.
3. In actuality, the closer we walk with Jesus, the more honest we are able to be about our sin, which exposes our need to be counseled by others. The Bible continually encourages us to seek counsel from those wiser than us. It is the fool who believes that counsel is not to be sought. Proverbs 11:14; 13:10; 15:22; and 24:6 are just a few verses that express the importance of having counselors in our lives.
4. When I speak of being pathetic, I do not mean on a vertical level. We are perfectly righteous in our relationship with God. It is our life on the horizontal level that I call pathetic as even our good works are considered nothing more than menstrual rags. "We have all become like one who is unclean, and all our righteous deeds are like a polluted garment. We all fade like a leaf, and our iniquities, like the wind, take us away" (Isa. 64:6).
5. Brennan Manning, *Lion and Lamb: The Relentless Tenderness of Jesus* (Grand Rapids: Chosen Books, 1986), 131–32.
6. Psalm 103:13–14.
7. Romans 5:8.
8. Nadia Bolz-Weber, *Pastrix* (New York: Jericho Books, 2013), 138–39.
9. John Eagan, *A Traveler toward the Dawn* (Chicago: Loyola University Press, 1990), xii.

Chapter 4 An Exposure That Leads to Freedom

1. Pless, *Handling the Word of Truth*, 13.
2. Lauren Larkin, "The Gospel Is Still the Gospel," *Dropping Keys* (blog). http://www.dropping-keys.com/the-gospel-is-still-the-gospel/.

Chapter 5 Romans 8:1 on Repeat

1. Tullian Tchividjian, *One Way Love: Inexhaustible Grace for an Exhausted World* (Colorado Springs: David C. Cook, 2013), 93.
2. Zac Hicks, "His Be the Victor's Name, " *His Be the Victor's Name*. Unbudding Fig Music, 2013.
3. Paul Zahl, *Who Will Deliver Us?: The Present Power of the Death of Christ* (New York: Seabury Press, 1983), 71.
4. Francis Spufford, *Unapologetic: Why, Despite Everything, Christianity Can Still Make Surprising Emotional Sense* (New York: HarperCollins, 2013), 130.
5. Ibid., 127.

Chapter 6 Stubborn Grace

1. Weezer, "Undone," *The Blue Album*. DGC Records, 1994. MP3.
2. Mike Yaconelli, *Messy Spirituality* (Grand Rapids: Zondervan, 2002, 2007), 158–59.
3. Steve Brown, *Scandalous Freedom* (New York: Howard Books, 2004), 113.

Chapter 7 Doubt Is Not a Dirty Word

1. Chad Bird, *Christ Alone*, 94.
2. In reality, I may or may not be sinning more, I just see it more clearly than when I was younger.
3. Spufford, *Unapologetic*, 21.
4. Martin Luther, *Luther: Letters of Spiritual Counsel*, ed. Theodore J. Tappert (Vancouver: Regent College Publishing, 2003), 86–7.
5. Barbara Duguid, *Extravagant Grace: God's Glory Displayed in Our Weakness* (Phillipsburg, NJ: P&R, 2013), 151–52.

Chapter 8 Living in Our Belovedness

1. Henri Nouwen, *Life of the Beloved: Spiritual Living in a Secular World* (New York: Crossroad, 1992), 33–35.
2. When I say fail, I mean that we have not done these things in thought, word, and deed. Every good work is tainted because we are not yet made perfect. (Well, it's tainted because we gather some sort of self-satisfaction from it, and it bloats our pride more. A truly good work is both spontaneous and unnoticed by the doer.) If we did manage to serve at the soup kitchen we may have found ourselves complaining inwardly in one way or another, or been prideful that we did something that so few are willing to do.
3. Robert Capon, *The Mystery of Christ . . . & Why We Don't Get It* (Grand Rapids: Eerdmans, 1993), 21.
4. Robert Capon, *Between Noon and Three: A Parable of Romance, Law, and the Outrage of Grace* (San Francisco: Harper & Row, 1982), 175.
5. Chad Bird, "Who Are You? Why Are You Here?", *Flying Scroll* (blog), February 13, 2015. https://birdchadlouis.wordpress.com/2015/02/13/who-are-you-why-are-you-here/.
6. Alan Jones, *Soul-Making* (San Francisco: Harper & Row, 1985), 145.
7. Brennan Manning, *The Ragamuffin Gospel* (Colorado Springs: Multnomah Books, 1990, 2000, 2005), 165.
8. If you are experiencing abuse, whether physical or emotional, please seek the help that you need. Grace is never an excuse for abuse. There are messes that require us to seek outside help from our pastor or a trained counselor.
9. Yes, I understand that having a mother who is a drug addict is not good for family life. We should all strive for healthy and safe environments in which to raise our kids. I am speaking of matters of the heart here.
10. Henri Nouwen, *Adam: God's Beloved* (Maryknoll, NY: Orbis Books, 2012), 42.

Chapter 9 Kissed by Grace

1. Yaconelli, *Messy Spirituality*, 41.
2. https://twitter.com/robert_f_capon/status/549396869336428545. Accessed on July 23, 2015.
3. Spufford, *Unapologetic*, 219.
4. Capon, *Between Noon and Three*, 119.

Kimm Crandall is a mother of four who is never short on examples of how God has flooded her with the excessive grace that the gospel brings. Kimm and Justin, her husband of nineteen years, serve at Valley Center Community Church. Kimm is the author of *Christ in the Chaos: How the Gospel Changes Motherhood* and founder of Dropping Keys Ministries.

Twitter: @KimmCrandall, @DroppingKeys_
Instagram: @KimmCrandall
Facebook: www.facebook.com/kimmcrandallauthor
kimmcrandall.com
dropping-keys.com

CONNECT WITH KIMM

Subscribe to her blog, send her a note, and read more at **KimmCrandall.com**.

  @KimmCrandall

  Kimm Crandall

LIKE THIS
BOOK?
Consider sharing it with others!

- Share or mention the book on your social media platforms. Use the hashtag **#BelovedMess**.

- Write a book review on your blog or on a retailer site.

- Pick up a copy for friends, family, or strangers! Anyone who you think would enjoy and be challenged by its message.

- Share this message on Twitter or Facebook. "**I loved #BelovedMess by @KimmCrandall//** kimmcrandall.com **@ReadBakerBooks**"

- Recommend this book for your church, workplace, book club, or class.

- Follow Baker Books on social media and tell us what you like.

 Facebook.com/ReadBakerBooks

 @ReadBakerBooks